Here's what the experts are saying about *Making 2 + 2 = 5*

"If you want a crisp 'how to' set of tools to increase productivity in your operation this is the book."

—Robert Janson, *Director*
Coopers & Lybrand L.L.P.

". . . offers practical insights and suggestions that would make average leaders good and good leaders better."

—Dr. David Ulrich, *Professor of Business*
University of Michigan

". . . reminded me of Harvey Penick's classic *Little Red Book* on golf, i.e., short, clear, practical tips on how to get the job done . . . a useful addition to every manager's bookshelf."

—Jon Katzenbach, *Director*
McKinsey & Company, Inc.

". . . distills many of the current best practices in these areas, and should be read by all managers concerned with improving their people and processes . . . a timely manifesto on the real cause and cures for under-performance in companies."

—Frank V. Cespedes, *Managing Partner*
The Center for Executive Development

"Jack Zenger's latest book is an extraordinary collection of commonsense wisdom. If managers and supervisors applied its practical advice, America's productivity would skyrocket beyond belief."

—Stephen J. Frangos, *President of Frangos Consulting and Author of* Team Zebra

"CEOs looking to run a company staffed with peak performers should get a copy of *Making 2 + 2 = 5* into the hands of every manager . . . puts high achievement within the reach of any organization."

—Charles Garfield, Ph.D.
Author of Second to None *and* Peak Performers

"Common sense uncommonly applied to the pursuit of productivity. Forget all the management buzzwords of the last decade, read the book and make something happen in your work group and organization. *Making 2 + 2 = 5* equals 2^{10}!"

—Frank Smith, *VP, Human Resource Development,*
REVLON

"Wow! A one-stop reference guide that cuts through management theories, fads, and buzzwords to the commonsense principles that boost productivity."

—*Jim Clemmer,* Author of Pathways to Performance *and* Firing on All Cylinders

"A real gem. I'm sometimes asked for one source on how to implement the management ideas I've written about. I now have the answer: Jack Zenger's book."

—*Bob Waterman,* Co-author of In Search of Excellence

". . . brings Jack Zenger's knowledge alive in a powerful, easy-to-understand and useful way."

—*Ken Blanchard,* Co-author of The One Minute Manager

". . . this excellent book is to help managers lead teams to greater productivity . . . a clearly written, down-to-earth and useful guide to increase wealth and creativity through productivity."

—*Warren Bennis, University Professor and Distinguished Professor of Business Administration, University of Southern California and Author of* Creative Collaboration

"Jack Zenger has written an efficient book for today's time-constrained leader . . . if an organizational leader just does half of what Jack prescribes, it'll quickly send the performance needle in the right direction."

—*Jim Shaffer, Principal*
Towers Perrin

". . . practical thoughts and actions that can actually be implemented as part of real work life."

—*Philip B. Crosby,* *Chairman*
Career IV, Inc.

". . . since your time is the most relevant factor in the equation, buy and read this book now so you and your constituents can boost your productivity before another day passes!"

—*Jim Kouzes,* *Co-author of* The Leadership Challenge and Credibility *and Chairman & CEO of The Tom Peters Group/Learning Systems*

Making
2 + 2 = 5

Making
$2 + 2 = 5$

22 Action Steps Leaders Take to Boost Productivity

John H. Zenger

IRWIN
Professional Publishing®
Burr Ridge, Illinois
New York, New York

Times Mirror
Higher Education Group

Library of Congress Cataloging-in-Publication Data
Zenger, John H.
    Making 2 + 2 = 5: 22 action steps leaders take to boost
productivity/John H. Zenger.
        p.   cm.
    Included index.
    ISBN 0–7863–1094–4
    1. Labor productivity.   2. Work groups.   I. Title.
HD57.Z429   1997
658.3′ 14—dc20   96–22738

Printed in the United States of America
1 2 3 4 5 6 7 8 9 0 QF 3 2 1 0 9 8 7 6

*To Mark, Robin, Roger, Todd, Kirk, Blake,
Lori, Mitchell, Drew, and Mike; who
along with their partners have become best
friends and a source of constant inspiration.*

Preface

Why I Wrote This Book

There were three distinct reasons why I wrote this book. They range from highly practical and organizational issues to philosophical, some would say spiritual, issues.

1 To Help Every Leader Improve the Productivity of a Work Group

This book gives practical prescriptions to leaders regarding steps they can take to improve the productivity of their work group. Because the quality movement prodded many companies to make great strides in both product and service quality, the big remaining issue now is productivity. It is of such paramount importance because it affects our nation's economic well-being, every company's success, and the career progress of every person who works for a living.

At the most basic level, this books provides 22 practical ways for the leader of any work group to help that group lift its level of productivity to a significantly higher level. It is not theoretical; it presents actionable ideas from research and corporate experience. Most people who lead will find valuable ideas inside this book that they can immediately put into action.

Everyone who works in large corporations has heard the cliche "work smarter, not harder." No one would quarrel with it. But we've generally failed to tell people *how* to do that. Worse yet, we've failed to recognize that many of the barriers to productivity are unwittingly the consequence of management practices and behavior. As Peter Drucker observed, "Much of what we call management consists of making it much more difficult for workers to do their job."

So this book helps leaders to teach their people how to work smarter.

2   To Propose a Major Turnabout in the Things Leaders Focus On

I have been troubled by the lack of attention to the issue of productivity. This book is a plea to all executives and managers to pay more attention to it.

Productivity is a leadership issue—you can do a great deal about it. I wanted to show that productivity can be improved without undue pain.

But it calls for leaders to reverse some of their past behavior. Ironically, in the past corporate leaders placed most of their emphasis on actions that would control the people and closed their eyes to issues of a dysfunctional corporate culture and to cumbersome work processes and systems.

I propose a reversal in that behavior. Leaders should be placing the greatest emphasis on fixing the culture and streamlining the work processes. They should leave to the front-line people the detailed ways of how to do their job and to execute those processes.

3   To Help Leaders Live More Effectively with the Conflicts and Contradictions of Modern Work Life

This book was also written to help the reader resolve a dilemma that faces a great number of people in our society. Do you live your life to make a real difference and maximize your contribution to society, or do you take a more selfish view of emphasizing enjoyment and comfort for yourself and family? I suspect I'm not alone in having wrestled with those competing values. Unable to choose one or the other, I've tried to find the proper balance in the middle.

The answer I have come to is simple. Given the job expectations and pressures of today's world, it is only by becoming extremely productive in the time you dedicate to work that you can have any time left for recreation and enjoyment.

We must find ways to free ourselves and those who work with us so that we have both time and resources to be with family, to enjoy nature, to serve in our communities, and to enjoy this life. Without that, our hard work has no purpose.

Increasing productivity on the job and fulfilling the basic purpose for which we were put here are in complete harmony.

John H. Zenger

Acknowledgments

My appreciation goes to the entire Irwin Professional Publishing staff. Jeffrey Krames has been a constant source of encouragement about this book; and Caroline Carney has overseen its development with enthusiasm and commitment. Special thanks also to Cindy Johansson, my remarkable assistant, who typed the manuscript and handled the administrative details that are necessary in writing a book, and did it with good humor and grace.

J. H. Z.

Contents

Part 3

RAISE THE BAR

Part 4

GIVE PEOPLE THE TOOLS TO PERFORM

Part 1

Prepare Yourself and Your Organization

"The single greatest challenge facing managers in the developed countries of the world is to raise the productivity of knowledge and service workers. This challenge, which will dominate the management agenda for the next several decades, will ultimately determine the competitive performance of companies."

Peter Drucker

The following chapters recommend steps to prepare an organization for transformation into a world-class company. Just as a painter prepares walls by filling cracks, sanding and priming, we need to prepare the organization. The first chapter describes the need for a personal change of attitude in how we view the groups and activities for which we are responsible. The second chapter describes the importance of communicating reality— holding up a mirror to the company so that people get an honest view of how things really are, with no rosy filters.

Preparation requires knowing exactly where you stand with customers. The third chapter describes how to discover your customers' current loyalty to your firm. How do they really feel about your products and services?

Chapter 4 describes your role in helping the organization develop a clear vision of what it should become in the future. But that's not something executives do in a vacuum. It demands many inputs from a variety of people in the organization.

Finally, preparation means rewarding the right things. The fifth chapter explains the process of getting the compensation plans of the company straightened out so that they're well understood, they're pushed down to the appropriate levels, and they reinforce the right behavior.

CHAPTER 1 Mind Your Own Business

"Management has no power,
management has only responsibility."

—Peter Drucker

Thoughts

There's lots of talk today about change. We're finally beginning to understand change and how to go about it. But talking about it in the abstract sometimes misses the point. Going bankrupt is a change. So is crashing into a concrete wall at 90 miles per hour. It helps to talk about the positive end results we're after: Dominating a market niche. Decreasing the time it takes to get a new product into the market. Increasing market share. It is the end state that's really important—and "change" is the abstract description of how you get there.

The end that this book focuses on is *productivity.* We've made huge strides in product quality and some improvements in service quality. Our biggest issue now is how to get more outputs from our inputs. How can we do more with less? The companies that are leading the pack are the ones that get higher productivity from their people than their competitors get. Some front runners are achieving 6 to 10 percent productivity improvement, while the firms around them are at 1 percent or declining in productivity.

The firms that increase productivity at a fast clip enjoy huge benefits. Their people are paid better. They eclipse competitors. The companies are comfortably profitable, so they can afford to invest in R&D or new market channels.

Their performance provides a "costless growth" to our economy, which in turn raises the living standard of the nation. High productivity also allows the United States to compete with countries whose wages are one-fifth of ours or less. For example, our productivity levels make our unit labor costs lower than Malaysia or the Philippines. Those are the reasons to focus on raising productivity.

The first step in getting there may sound strange. Simply stated, you have to be willing to accept complete responsibility for the productivity of the groups or teams you manage. No excuses.

Three facts stand out about productivity in most organizations.

1   *Productivity is at a fairly low level and most managers know it.*

I've conducted many management seminars during my active years in business. I would often ask executives and managers how productive they thought they personally were. I'd also ask them how productive they thought the team or group they managed was. I proposed a simple yardstick. If 100 percent was the level that people could sustain over a long period of time without physical or mental harm, what score would they give themselves personally and what score would they give their group?

The number that consistently came up was 60 percent. I'm the first to admit that it was unscientific, but I was amazed at the consensus. It told me that we had a long way to go and that most of us knew it. What was even more amazing, however, was that no one felt compelled to do anything about it. They acted as if it were out of their hands. One executive told me he knew the organization could produce twice as much as it currently did if there were some compelling reason.

2   *Productivity varies widely among people who are doing the same job and getting paid nearly the same.*

Professors Hunter, Schmidt, and Judiesch have studied the productivity of individuals. They analyzed 81 studies that covered tens of thousands of people.

The following table summarizes what they found. The basic message is simple: People vary widely in how productive they are, and again managers basically ignore it. One study of software programmers showed that the high performers were 16 times as productive as the lowest performers. The table shows the huge differences in the more complex jobs.[1]

Complexity of Job	Top 1% vs. Bottom 1%	Top 1% vs. Average
Low	300%	52% more
Medium	1,200%	85% more
High	Infinite	127% more

There used to be a saying: "A fair day's work for a fair day's pay." There was an unwritten contract that said to workers, "If you'll be obedient, follow orders, not embarrass management, and not rock the boat, then we'll leave you alone and let you work at a moderate pace, doing things the same way you did years ago. We'll stay off your back." Well, those days are gone.

I believe there are many things a leader can do to change that, to get the lower performers up to at least average and the average ones up with some of the leaders. That's *your* responsibility.

3   *Companies don't have any systematic process in place to improve productivity over time.*

We act as if our performance were getting better when it really isn't. Employees want higher salaries and better benefits, and we give them. But we haven't explained that we can't pay for those endless increases unless one of three things happens. We must (1) pay for them with inflation, (2) decrease the shareholders' return, or (3) generate higher productivity.

---

[1] John F. Hunter, Frank L. Schmidt, and Michael Judiesch; "Individual Differences in Output Variability as a Function of Job Complexity," *Journal of Applied Psychology*, 75, No. 1, pp. 28–42.

If there's inflation, then you can afford salary increases, if you raise prices to cover your higher costs. (It's more complicated than that, but that's the basic idea.) But you and I both know that getting a 4 percent salary increase in an economy that's experiencing 4 percent inflation isn't going to improve anyone's living standard by much.

There are three major stakeholders of every company: customers, employees, and shareholders. (*CEO* is a nice memory device to remember our important stakeholders.) Companies get into trouble when they ignore or shortchange any one of those three. You must constantly attend to them all if you plan to succeed in the long run. Becoming less profitable to increase employee compensation has serious limits and can't go on for long.

The best alternative is for us to increase the firm's productivity. Then the company can increase pay and benefits without damaging its performance for the shareholders or shortchanging customers. Everyone wins.

Fewer than 20 percent of organizations have any organized plan to improve the productivity of their work force.

The organizations I've worked with have marketing plans, sales plans, facilities plans, and capital expenditure plans, but no plan to improve the productivity of their most important resource, people. Yet they religiously budget 3 to 5 percent salary increases and benefits improvements. The numbers don't work out. It's crazy.

A study conducted by McKinsey & Co. showed that 85 percent of the variables affecting productivity were internal to the firms studied. Real business leaders accept responsibility to constantly improve the productivity and performance of their group. It's part of their job to bring about positive change.

"The gap is the problem—not labor, not a lack of new technology or enough capital investment. Management has simply created an organizational environment that is hostile to productivity."

Jay Hall, president of Teleometrics and professor at University of Texas

Things to Do

Accepting responsibility for the performance of any group has many elements. Let me suggest some specific things you can do.

1   Don't duck responsibility by saying that you delegated to others. Nor can you say, "We're a team and they are responsible." I believe in empowering people. I believe in teams. But if you are the manager, accept responsibility.

2   Pass on all the credit and praise when things go well and accept all of the responsibility when things go badly. The worst managers I know do just the opposite. They take credit when things go well and blame subordinates when things go badly.

3   Do whatever you must to have the group perform well. That may mean terminating poor performers, reorganizing work, or outsourcing. There are many painful decisions to implement. But that's what being responsible means.

4   Don't blame upper management for controversial decisions, even if you didn't agree with them. If you didn't agree, you should have spoken up. If you spoke up and didn't convince those above you, then you owe them your support. Never say, "Well, we're canceling the project, but I don't think we should." Or, "Well, here's your salary increase, but I put you in for a lot more." That's irresponsible.

5   Do whatever a customer needs that's within reason. Organizations exist to serve customers, and they should never get less than your best.

6   Don't let things fall into the cracks. One of the biggest flaws in many organizations is that managers shrug their shoulders and say, "Well, that wasn't our job." If you can reach it or touch it in any way, and you think it is going to fall, it is your job.

7   Do things for which there is no immediate reward, such as developing your subordinates. Responsible leaders do what is best for the organization and their people—even if there is no short-term gain for them.

8   Communicate your intense dedication and your sense of urgency to have your group succeed. Make sure everyone knows that.

9   Hold people accountable for the things they promised to do. If someone misses a deadline, don't just overlook it. I'm not suggesting you drop a ton of bricks on them, but you should discuss why the deadline was missed and how they can avoid that problem in the future.

10   Be willing to put yourself out—to sacrifice—if it will help the performance of the group.

"Isn't there something we can appear to be doing?"

Henry Cabot Lodge, in a letter to Theodore Roosevelt during the 1902 coal strike.

Tips & Afterthoughts

Taking responsibility is an attitude you have about your work group's performance, your relationship with the people who report to you, and your relationship with upper management.

You know leaders are acting responsibly when they feel pain if the group's performance is below budget. You also know it when they are willing to put themselves out—by more travel or longer hours—to get needed work done.

A personal anecdote:

I had just finished college, and I was debating going on to graduate school versus going to work. Through a relative I was offered a job where I could make a lot of money, but it was narrow and provided little personal or long-term career growth. My older brother took me aside and said, "Jack, you're thinking about taking a job that will pay you lots of money for now, but you'll never become what you could become if you do that."

That statement changed my life. I decided to go on to graduate school, and my brother was right. I was able to accomplish a great deal more.

Every manager has the obligation to ensure that his or her work group does their best, that they achieve all that is possible for them to achieve. Leaders need to be like a coach who sees young athletes capable of far more than they are doing today and who can never rest until the athletes have performed to their potential. That's really what's behind this "responsibility" thing. It means making sure that the groups for which you are responsible are doing all that they are capable of doing—nothing less.

"We firmly believe that responsibility for productivity decline lies on the shoulders of management. It has been reactive, not proactive, in coping with the impact of external factors on internal productivity."

Keith A. Bolte, author of "Intel's War for White Collar Productivity" in Human Resources Productivity II, *Executive Enterprises, 1985.*

CHAPTER 2 Be a Truth Teller—and Listener

"In order to cope with reality, one must know what reality is."

—*Douglas McGregor, author of The Human Side of Enterprise, 1960.*

Thoughts

Open the floodgates of communication. Be a truth teller. Let people know how things really are and what the long-term consequences of current performance will be. Make the status quo unacceptable.

Leading is all about making things improve. Managers are quite able to preserve the status quo. Leaders catapult things to a new level. One of the first steps is to help everyone see that what's going on currently is not satisfactory. Leaders need to make sure everyone in the organization understands reality. The world needs truth tellers.

But to be a truth teller, you must know what is really going on in the organization. That can happen only if you're willing to listen to the truth.

> After the new president was appointed head of one of the major stock exchanges, his colleagues gathered in the board room to congratulate him on his new position. One raised his glass and with a big smile on his face said, "Here's to the last time you ever heard the truth from your colleagues."

To get the truth—the reality of the organization—requires some hard listening. It's hard because you have to go out after it. It seldom seeks you out. Worse yet, there are barriers that grow like coral reefs in every organization. They filter out candor and straight talk on the way up. Your employees have been taught to respect authority, so that means laundering their comments to make them bland and painless. Some may worry about being punished for speaking truth.

> **"He that would speak the truth must have one foot in the stirrup."**
>
> *Turkish proverb*

That means you have to ask penetrating questions. Then wait. Don't fill in the silences. Be willing to listen to things that make you uncomfortable. These messages will often be troubling. In many cases, you'll think they reflect badly on you. In other cases, foolish things will be happening that you would have expected others to fix by now.

But if you want to learn reality, try not to let your irritation show through. An angry response will slam the door on any further information. Even if the information makes your blood pressure rise 10 points, your ability to appear calm will determine whether or not you get more information.

"That hourly workers might have significant ideas on how to improve productivity, and operations generally, is a notion quite foreign in many American executive circles, where it is assumed that only gripes and grievances emanate from the factory floor and that such is the total content of employee comments.

In 30 years of consulting experience and face-to-face interviews with about 500,000 hourly workers, I have found there is a gold mine of information in their comments."

A. A. Imberman, Consultant

Things to Do

1 Have periodic one-on-one interviews with colleagues to learn their views of what's going well, what's not going well, and what needs to be started.

2 Protect confidences. If someone tells you something in confidence, you must absolutely not divulge it. When someone gives you an important piece of information, make it a practice to say, "Is it OK if I use this information you've given me and tell people where it came from?" Or "May I use the information if I don't attribute it to you?" People will usually agree to one of those. If not, and they've asked you not to act on the information, then make it an unswerving practice to honor their request.

3 Get information from a variety of sources. In addition to your interviews, get

- financial data over time, especially performance against budget.

- observations from the leaders of other departments.

- views from outside suppliers or customers who interact with your group.

Once you've collected this information and thoroughly digested it, you can come to your own informed opinions. Now you're ready to start communicating your views to those around you.

4 Present charts and graphs that describe the performance of your group over time. Show the percentage growth in compensation over that same time. Compare that to the growth in profitability. Display measures of productivity such as sales per salesperson, sales per employee, hires per human resources (HR) staff member, orders per person in order entry, or items shipped per factory worker. Portray what's happened over time. Explain that some companies have been recording a 5 to 10 percent growth in productivity every year for the past five years and that the organization's ability to grow and pay higher salaries is based on your group's ability to produce more per person.

This should be a balanced scorecard. Create a permanent bulletin board to display the best measures of your group's performance.

Baldrige Award winner Solectron sponsors a weekly meeting to review detailed performance data for every plant. Anyone in the company can attend. When you sit in on this meeting, you are impressed with the level of detail that is being reported and with Solectron's willingness to make it available to anyone who wants to attend.

---

5   Tell everything you know about organizations that are outperforming yours. Often people inside an organization are like horses in blinders running in a race. It's easy to think you're doing really well if you have no idea how anyone else is doing. One of your jobs as the leader is to be the antenna to the outside world, reporting what's really going on out there.

6   Tell your employees where you see inefficiency (without pointing fingers at any individuals). Most inefficiency and lack of productivity in organizations comes in the hand-offs from one person or one group to another. It's caused by bad processes and systems. Point them out, but be careful not to berate any one person.

7   Explain where you see big opportunities for improvement. If you've examined the operations of your group, chances are you have some ideas about where things could get better. Turn a searchlight on important areas that need to be fixed, and then let the group decide how to make them better.

8   Commend things that are going well. Don't be one-sided in your communications. Be a cheerleader for the progress that's being made. But never forget that your main task is to shake people out of their rut.

"He goes to the real people—the worker bees—to see where problems are. He knows it's these people, not the corporate fat cats, who know the truth."

Don Frey, professor at Northwestern, speaking of Jack Welch of General Electric.

Tips & Afterthoughts

How do you find out the truth and tell it?

Talk to people one on one. Nothing can substitute for personal contact in organizations. Have meetings with your entire work group. Help them see the need for immediate change. Use the e-mail system. Leave messages on voice mail for everyone at least once a month. Write memos. Have breakfast meetings. Invite people in for informal chats.

Communicating companies contain strange sights. Bulletin boards with elaborate scrap-rate charts, productivity measures, and yields. Easels on which people have written the "question of the day" for which they're seeking an answer. Letters from customers separated under "Agony" and "Ecstasy" signs.

People change and find ways to improve the group's output when they recognize that the current situation can't go on. You are the watcher on the tower reporting on the hostile forces around you that threaten your safety and security. Usually there are people who share your views. Identify the other truth tellers and get them to speak up in meetings.

Normally it is only when you are communicating three or four times as much as you think necessary that your people get the message. When you've said the same thing for the 25th time, then people get the message.

Most managers think they're communicating adequately: but at the same time, the people who report to them think they're being kept in the dark. Normally it is only when you are communicating three or four times as much as you think necessary that your people get the message. Phrase the message in vivid, memorable words. Make it simple. Keep repeating it over and over. You'll get sick of saying it long before the people around you get sick of hearing it.

Examples, stories, and anecdotes make the point better than abstract talk. Insert appropriate real-life incidents that illustrate your concerns. You've got to connect to hearts and heads at the same time.

Create in your colleagues the desire to improve and change without making them feel like they're failures and you're blaming them. That's why it's mandatory that you describe *what's* going wrong, not *who's* doing wrong.

Don't be afraid to give people abundant financial and statistical information. There are smart people who will understand that information every bit as well as you do. When they see the numbers, they'll support your concerns about change and know what to do to make better numbers.

I've worked with a few executives (most often the ones in the financial end) who worried about some employee calling a stockbroker with confidential information about the company. But my experience has been that when leaks occur, they usually come from attorneys or loose-lipped outside financial advisors. I have never known firsthand of an employee leaking information to the street.

Information is food for the organization's soul.

Communicating the reality and seriousness of your current situation is a vital step in preparing to improve things. Excellent information is food for the organization's soul. Until you provide it, you'll never succeed. You'll make changes that only you believe in, and your people will resist in a thousand ways—or worse yet, engage in malicious compliance.

You have to help them understand what concerns you. Now, you may feel it more deeply, and you may be the one leading the charge. But at all costs avoid being the platoon sergeant who is forging a river 60 yards ahead of the group while the privates are scratching their heads and wondering why that nut is out there all alone.

We're starting out with the preparation necessary to get the organization ready to climb out of its rut. You can't push it out. But you can help everyone see why they need to pull it out.

Two Harvard Business School professors did an extensive study of numerous companies in 16 industries and concluded that nearly all of them "lacked sufficient flexibility and adaptability to be economically successful in the long run."[2] That's a professor's way of saying that all but a few organizations are in serious trouble and that unless they change their culture, they are going to be out of business. That's a sobering message.

---

[2]John P. Kotter and James L. Heskett, *Corporate Culture and Performance* (New York: Free Press, 1992), p. 150.

CHAPTER 3 Turn Hostages into Partners

"Service leadership is all about unnatural market share, i.e., getting a piece of somebody else's pie."
—*Karl Albrecht, author and consultant*

Thoughts

This action step involves measuring your customers' loyalty and turning companies or people that often feel like hostages into loyal partners.

It's a cliché that a business exists to serve customers. In the last few years we've expanded that notion. Now we say that every department inside every company has internal customers. So whether you're in sales or customer service, finance or human resources, you've got customers. But we're going to focus on our ultimate, external customer, the one who writes a check for our product or services.

Total quality management has contributed much to our understanding. The TQM movement developed a technique called quality function deployment, which assigned numerical values to customer attributes and compared them to descriptive information about a company's product characteristics.

Market research firms have developed a similar sophisticated technique to plot the trade-offs that customers use to choose one product or service over another and then to see how your firm's products compare to that plot of trade-offs. For example, does the customer value uniqueness more than price, or product quality over ease of accessibility? By understanding how the customer views these trade-offs and how your products stack up on this analysis, you can better understand why customers may or may not be loyal to you.

Nearly everyone travels on airlines, so they are a good illustration of an important point. If you go back to the airline records in 1987 and analyze customer complaint data kept by the Department of Transportation, you'll see that of the five major airlines that had the worst records for customer complaints, two are now liquidated and three are in bankruptcy. On the other hand, of the five airlines that had the best records for customer satisfaction, all are still in operation and financially healthy, despite their tough, competitive industry. Satisfied customers (or more importantly, loyal customers) are what keep organizations in business.

"Look at our balance sheet. On the asset side, you can still see so-and-so many aircraft worth so-and-so many billions. But it's wrong; we are fooling ourselves. What we should put on the asset side is, last year SAS carried so-and-so many happy passengers. Because that's the only asset we've got— people who are happy with our service and are willing to come back and pay for it once again.

The only thing that counts is a satisfied customer."

Jan Carlzon, president of Scandinavian Airlines

Things to Do

1 Measure how your customers feel about your current level of service and/or the quality of your products. I'm astonished at how few companies have any quantitative measure of this. Some have feelings and impressions, but they vary from person to person. No one knows who is right. Organizations that measure the cost of their product down to 0.001 cent per part often haven't the vaguest notion of how many of their customers think the company provides good service, or how they would rate its service in comparison to competitors'.

One researcher discovered that asking customers how they "feel" about your organization is a better predictor of their future with you than merely asking them to rate numerically the quality of your product or your service. Loyalty has a lot to do with feelings. To measure it, you can use an outside group that specializes in measuring customer satisfaction, or you can create your own questionnaire and polling techniques.

2 Find out from your customers if they believe your service has been improving or deteriorating in the last six months.

3 Calculate what a loyal customer is worth to you over two or three years. That means locating several of them and examining your records for what they purchased and how much net profit per year their purchases generated.

4 Determine *how* loyal your current customers are. Being satisfied is important, but the real issue is whether customers are going to continue to buy from you or defect to a competitor. Find out what it would take to have a competitor lure away your customer. I've found most customers are brutally honest about telling you what it would take to pull them away. Ask the direct question.

5   Analyze how many customers you've lost each year for the past few years and how many you've added. Can you calculate the cost of adding a new client? What's the cost of losing one?

6   Call 10 clients you've lost and find out why. Every executive should get involved in doing this. Get together and pool your data—and find out the common themes or reasons for losing these valuable assets.

7   Write down the mechanism you now have for getting the voices of customers directly, unfiltered, into your executive decision-making process. If you don't have one (and most companies don't), then figure out how to make it happen.

The CEO of a ski resort met with 600 employees in 30 meetings during one winter. His question to the employees was "What's the customer saying to you? I'm not asking you what you think—I'd like to hear that later, but right now I want to know what the customers think."

Tips & Afterthoughts

I'm always amazed that despite the high salaries and compensation given salespeople in most organizations, the company leaders make absolutely no concerted effort to capture the information the salespeople collect on a daily basis from being face to face with customers.

Maybe its because the sale reps are "in our face" over so many little issues that we get numbed, and we discount their suggestions and feedback. But next to making sales for us, the most valuable contribution of a field force is their constant gathering of market intelligence. I fear most organizations are reaping only half the value of their field force.

One big payoff from measuring how your customers feel about your company is that it becomes your baseline measurement to see if you are really improving customer service.

I've been in companies where auditors swarmed over us once a year to make sure every nickel was accounted for, and at the same time customers were defecting in droves. No one said a word. The customer base, measured by both retention and current levels of satisfaction, is one of the most valuable assets you have (along with your work force and your product technology).

A final thought: Companies are beginning to realize the importance of good customer service. What many don't seem to fully comprehend is the direct relationship between how you treat your employees and how they in turn deal with customers. The research is really clear. If you run roughshod over employees and treat them in a demeaning way, you can't expect them to flip a switch in their heads and suddenly treat an outside customer with courtesy and respect. They give what they get.

I was giving a speech in a New York hotel. I got to the room early and the waiters were setting up the tables. I watched one waiter get royally chewed out by his supervisor for something he had forgotten to do. It seemed trivial to me and the treatment harsh. As luck would have it, he was the waiter for the head table. As he walked by, I asked if he could find some butter for our end of the table. He looked up and snarled, "Can't you see I'm busy right now. I'll get around to it when I can!"

I understood perfectly. He was giving what he got. How your firm manages people is a major determinant of the quality of service you give your customers.

CHAPTER 4 Lead a Dream Team

"Where there is no vision the people perish."
—*Proverbs 29:18*

Thoughts

If you are reading this book, you are probably a member of a leadership team for some organization. One of the first things a leadership team must do is to create excitement and enthusiasm within every employee. That happens when people sign up for something bigger than they are, something that inspires their best efforts.

Forgive this philosophical detour, but everyone needs to have meaning and purpose in his or her life. Because we spend so many hours at work, for many people if their work has no meaning or purpose, then their life is devoid of meaning. As the old story goes, the person who sees his job as cutting stone into two-foot squares is usually less productive and less fulfilled than the one who sees himself as an important part of a team of artisans building a cathedral.

When Hewlett Packard executives choose people to head up operations, they basically look for two things: first, people who are technically competent, and second, people who can inspire and enthuse the people who work alongside them.

To create this inspiration, leaders must be able to articulate a vision that captures people's hearts and minds. They must paint a picture that is better than what existed in the past. They must do what a good architect does—envision a building that doesn't exist.

Then design it, engineer it, and oversee its construction. Beyond skill, they must have the ability to get others to share their vision of the future. They get people to believe in it, commit to it, and become convinced that it will happen under their leadership.

I've watched outstanding leaders do that. They paint a vivid picture of where this project could lead. They explain how it can benefit our society, how large it will grow, the technical breakthroughs the group can achieve, and the excitement of creating an organization that will treat people the way they all want to be treated themselves. Then finally they get around to talking about some of the financial rewards that may come from this venture.

They allow people around them to create the details. They are open to inputs from secretaries and assemblers. Intuitively they know this is the only way to build commitment. Everyone comes to feel he or she has had a say in shaping this vision of the future. Then the leader writes it down in words everyone can relate to. The key is that everyone in the organization feels like an owner of the vision. Everyone can repeat it in a one- or two-sentence conversation in an elevator ride between the fourth and fifth floor. If it gets long and convoluted, it doesn't mean anything.

The people in your organization need to see that you, the leadership team, are absolutely committed to this vision. They need to hear you talk about it often. They need to see you live it. They must see you use it as the touchstone for every key decision. You must hold everyone in the organization accountable for using the mission/vision/values statement as the basis for every important decision.

If you have a manager whose personal behavior is out of harmony with your core values and direction, no matter how good he or she is at making the numbers, your organization's character will be seriously challenged. As Jack Welsh, chairman of GE, puts it, "That becomes the acid test of the organization, and you have no alternative but to fire these people."

I know you've heard this before, but I'm amazed that roughly half of all companies haven't bothered to develop any kind of a mission or vision statement. What a waste! That's like living in a building wired with electricity and never bothering to turn on the switch. People get turned on when they're clear about where they're going and why they're doing what they've been asked to do.

Things to Do

1   Talk to lots of people inside your organization. Ask them why they think the organization exists. What is its purpose in society? What distinguishes it from other organizations? Why should people work hard to make it succeed? Where could it go? What could it do for society?

2   Where will the organization be five years from now? Where should it be? Get many different views.

3   What kind of culture should you be seeking to create? The evidence is that the best companies get built on the premise of making a good organization, not because of some new technology and product idea. Sure, some companies are all about product, but the larger, longer-lasting institutions have been built the other way around.

   Once you discover what others think about those questions, you can add your own ideas and beliefs and fine- tune the vision. Then as a team effort create a vision and mission statement for your group.

4   Articulate the vision. Get it written down with the help of those around you. Use the most action-packed language possible.

5   Talk about the vision frequently. Refer back to it as the compass by which all important decisions are made. Let everyone know that the vision/mission statement is a serious document that you will use as you make decisions. Never get bored giving the stump speech on the vision/mission statement.

6   Make certain that the vision/mission statement is clear to people. All the terms should be clear and unambiguous. The vision/mission statement should describe what you *won't* be as well as what you will be, if there is confusion about that now.

7   Make the vision statement a living set of ideas. People must know that you and others in leadership roles will work hard to make it real. It must serve as a bridge from the reality of today to the possibilities of tomorrow.

8   Remove every distraction, every byway, every barrier to your group's achieving that mission. Ask your people to identify those distractions.

Tips & Afterthoughts

It helps many people to understand that the mission statement of an organization answers the question *why.* "Why do we exist? Why are we engaged in this project?" That's different from what we're striving to be and do in the future.

Visions and goals often evolve. Values don't. They are the principles that guide your daily conduct—things like integrity, service to customers, and respect for employees.

Accept the fact that one of your key roles is to guard and protect the vision and the values. Keep them visible and protect them from those who would muddy the direction with short-term, half-baked objectives.

Financial goals are not a vision. They ignite only a few people at the top of the organization or those who have big equity interests. They don't describe why people down in the trenches should work longer hours and give their all. Most members of our society are turned on by causes that go beyond making money.

Witness the huge role of nonprofit organizations in our society.

> "Half of all American adults work for at least three hours a week as volunteers— about 90 million people. That is the largest single segment of our labor force. The business sector can learn a great deal from the nonprofit, which has learned to make volunteers productive. Volunteers know why they are there and what the task is that needs to be accomplished. The moment a nonprofit stops hammering away at the mission, the volunteers drift away. A powerful vision and mission do encourage people to serve."
>
> *Peter Drucker*

Mason Haire, a distinguished professor of behavioral science at Berkeley, used an instructive metaphor. He rejected the idea that you or I can motivate anyone to do anything, any more than we can *grow* plants. He talked about how people often say they grow vegetables or grow roses, but no one can force a seed to grow or make a slip of a plant send out roots and flourish. All we can do is to create a good environment in which the plant or seed grows itself. We can give it water, sunshine, optimal temperatures, and proper fertilizer. That's all! Most of the time, given those circumstances, plants grow. But not always. And when they do, we should be clear that we did not cause that minor miracle to happen. We merely provided the environment or the context.

Leaders are in exactly that same circumstance. We don't motivate people. We don't make them productive. We create environments in which they can be productive. The odds of people being really productive are very high if we create the right environment. But we should never lose sight of the fact that productivity is something that comes from within them. Our job is to create an environment that unleashes that enormous potential within them.

A clear vision and mission is an important element of the culture that only we can provide. Many elements of making an organization successful can be supplied by the front-line associates. These people can (and do) pick up many things that management drops or that bad systems create. But they can't create the vision and the values of the organization. They count on their leaders for that.

CHAPTER 5 Pay to Play

"Productivity creates the pool of wealth from which salaries and wages are paid. It must go up or real incomes can't improve."

—*Peter Drucker*

"It is not the employer who pays wages—he only handles the money. It is the product that pays wages."

—*Henry Ford*

Thoughts

There's been a profound evolution in the nature of our work force in the past 50 years. It's evolved from a childlike group through adolescence and is well on its way to adulthood.

Childhood

Sixty years ago, we hired people, paid them, managed them, and took care of them after retirement like a benevolent (or sometimes harsh) parent dealing with children. Everything was cut and dried. People punched time clocks and sometimes had to ask permission to go to the bathroom. Pay was for a job, and there was an hourly rate for that job, with not much variation for tenure or performance. Raises were annual cost-of-living increases given to everybody. Organizations were highly centralized, and autocratic managers controlled everything tightly. Training was largely technical. Little thought was given to the development of people's general skills to communicate or solve problems. Management wanted the front-line people to do what they were told, speak when spoken to, keep their noses clean, not rock the boat, and never infringe on management prerogatives.

Adolescence

In the 1960s we began to encourage people to speak up. Organizations became more decentralized. Pay shifted to a merit system, with incentives for better personal performance. Profit-sharing and Scanlon-type plans became popular. In the 1970s organizations developed more flexible benefits, often giving people some choices in a "cafeteria" benefit program. Employees were allowed to deal directly with the external providers. Working hours became more flexible, and accommodations were made for working mothers to modify their daily work pattern. Training was technical and job related but also included some "soft skills," like communicating and problem solving, that could be used in many situations both on and off the job. Lateral movement in the organization became acceptable as a career path. "What's my next promotion?" was no longer the only legitimate approach.

Adulthood

Today, we tell people they are managing their own career. There's no unseen hand guiding them through the company. They're responsible for their own retirement. We let them read their own "personnel file" and make them responsible for ensuring that their own records are accurate. They can check on the status of their pension or 401(k) plan by calling a toll-free number any time of day. There are many more choices of benefits, and people select which medical plan they prefer. Jobs are posted so everyone has a chance to apply. Telecommuting and job sharing are more common. Hiring decisions involve not just managers, but members of the team with whom the individual will be working. Pay is based on knowledge, competencies, and skills. The movement is toward a few broad pay bands, rather than multiple salary grades in fine distinctions. Time off for vacation, holidays, sick leave and other personal needs is often pooled, so people can take time off without having to lie to their employer about the reason. Performance feedback comes from many sources, among them peers, subordinates, customers, and even suppliers. Development is more self-paced. People are more responsible for their own education and for keeping current with the latest technology.

Impact on Pay

Nowhere is this new relationship between the company and its employees more evident than in pay practices. Where once there was one universal compensation system, some companies now have five dozen, each designed for a unique group in a unique situation. Because employees are now being viewed as responsible adults, companies are implementing a new philosophy, basically: We want you to share the risk of business fortunes with us. In good times, we'll pay you well—because we can afford to. In bad times, your pay will be cut back. We also recognize that if you have a stake in our success, you'll be more inclined to bring your head and heart to work along with your hands.

Indeed, workers are coming to realize that their future is so much at stake that they want to share some of the key decisions with upper-level executives.

Today, variable pay is booming. Over two-thirds of medium-size and large companies have some incentive or variable pay for people other than executives. Of companies of all sizes, about one-third have variable pay plans. They've learned to give splendid rewards at periodic intervals to people who are in a position to make-or-break the firm.

The best way to keep loyalty in a man's heart is to keep money in his purse.

Irish Proverb

Things to Do

1   Agree that you're going to set up a performance-based pay plan in your organization, and that you'll do it with the help of the people (not *to* them).

2   Create unique pay plans for different groups. Monsanto, for example, has 60 different plans in operation today. I know relatively small companies with nine plans in operation. Todd Zenger, a professor at Washington University in St. Louis, has shown that a pay plan's impact on performance increases approximately 20 percent for each level you move down in the organization. Compensation plans get more effective as the size of the group gets smaller. No wonder companywide profit-sharing plans in place for more than a year or two have little long-term effect on performance.

The point is to make sure that the compensation system drives what you want people to do. One approach is to look at the key objectives your people have for the year. Then one by one ask, "What is the consequence to them of doing or not doing that?" You'll probably discover that there are no rewards or punishments (in the broadest sense of that word) for achieving or not achieving those objectives.

Then review the behavior displayed by some workers that drives management nuts and ask, "What are the rewards to people for doing those things?" You may be surprised to find that there are usually subtle, unintended rewards for their behavior.

3   Involve the people in designing the plans. Have them help
     select the measures you'll use. They'll make sure the
     measures are simple, understandable, and reasonable. As a
     principle, don't ever hold people accountable for things
     over which they have no control. That's precisely why
     companywide profit-sharing plans fall into disrepute. The
     average worker can't make a big impact on the corporation's
     profits. But when you design a plan for the immediate
     group in which he or she works, suddenly that worker has a
     great deal of influence, if not control, over what happens.

     Get people highly involved in designing their own
     compensation plans. They know what they can change and
     what they can't. Keep the measures few in number and
     simple, perhaps three or four. If you can't explain it to a
     new employee while you're standing in the cafeteria line—
     it's too complicated.

     I realize that many managers think it is insane to involve
     people in designing their own compensation. They fear
     they'll greedily design unreasonable plans that management
     could never live with. I recall having those feelings. Stop
     worrying! If people have the right information and clear
     ground rules on which to operate (such as total
     compensation can not be more than x percent of sales), you
     needn't lose sleep over them designing their own
     compensation plans.

4   Implement the plans gradually. Don't have people get hurt
     by a new plan, unless it is the consequence of their reduced
     performance. Some firms run parallel accounting during
     the first 12 to 18 months of a new plan to ensure that
     people aren't being harmed by it.

5   Keep the targets fluid. Make some change, albeit a small
     one, in the plan each year so that people know that things
     can and will change. As new technology comes along or
     new work processes are implemented, the compensation

plans have to change. But don't punish the people who helped develop new work processes. Ensure that they are handsomely rewarded for their innovation and initiative.

6   Periodically revisit the plans to be certain they're yielding the intended result. For example, one company gave incentives to workers if there were no lost-time accidents reported in a month. You can guess how smart workers reacted to that. They coerced their co-workers who were legitimately injured into not reporting it. Stories were told of workers coming in with high fevers and of two workers carrying a co-worker in on a stretcher so he could punch in.

Tips & Afterthoughts

Compensation has taken a bad rap from management scholars and behavioral scientists. Traditionally they've said it isn't all that important because people worked for lots of other things besides money.

Adequate compensation lets you peacefully click off the light as you go to sleep, but it doesn't necessarily make you click your heels as you head for work. It seldom makes up for gross defects in your job. But when the other elements of a job are solidly in place, compensation becomes a powerful force to shape behavior.

People do work for lots of reasons, but money is the system of counters that we use in this game we call business, and it has meaning far beyond what those dollars will buy. When I see groups really bust their tails to make some challenging objective, most often there is some incentive for that terrific performance. Don't sell compensation short as a major driving force.

It works because it treats the front-line people the same way we treat executives. It makes part of their pay variable, so that when things go well they get more, and when things aren't doing well they feel the pain.

I'd recommend that you give some or all of raises in the form of added incentive pay. Rather than cutting people's salary, you just make all of the additions variable. But make the curve steep so that when things are going well, the employees do really well. Isn't that the behavior you want to reward? If you want higher productivity, then reward it and see what happens.

Allied Signal tied annual increases directly to increasing productivity. A 6 percent increase in productivity provided for a 3 percent salary increase, and a 9 percent increase in productivity generated a 6 percent salary increase. Anything less than a 6 percent productivity increase produced only a 2 percent salary increase that year.

If you have areas where teams are being held responsible for certain activities, then have incentives at the team level. You certainly don't want compensation to drive a team apart.

Be careful that incentive systems don't create competition between people or groups. Systems should always be based on beating a standard or a past number, never on one person or one team beating another. Such zero-sum systems are extremely destructive.

The companies that have installed variable pay plans have found that they more than pay for themselves. They're worth all the effort it takes to design and manage them.

Part 2

Shed Your Past

"Let us not go over the old ground, let us rather prepare for what is to come."

Marcus Tullius Cicero (106–43 B.C.)

The next five chapters describe a series of steps designed to leave behind the old ways of doing things in preparation for the new. Chapter 6 deals with bureaucracy, the mortal enemy of all business enterprise, and what organizations can do to eradicate its worst features. Chapter 7 describes an improvement process that's a sure-fire way to begin an organizational transformation.

Chapter 8 deals with the excruciating issue of handling poor performance. Chapter 9 moves on to streamlining the way work gets done in the organization, emphasizing the horizontal structure over the vertical one. The final chapter describes how organizations are being flattened out.

These are the steps you must take to rid your organization of its past and begin the process of renewal and transformation.

Waste

The fundamental issue that each of these chapters addresses is how organizations can become more efficient and eliminate waste. For that to happen, the leaders must develop a visceral hatred of waste. It destroys organizations. The extent of it inside most organizations is incredible. We laugh about government waste, and it *is* shameful. But no organization is immune.

Waste comes in many forms: People doing unnecessary things. (Like banks that process deposit slips when there is really no reason for them.) People making mistakes and having to do something over again. (Any time you have to rework something, there's been waste.) People not doing anything at all. (Playing computer games on the job or just goofing off instead of using their time to produce anything of value for the organization.) The waste of raw materials and supplies.

As leaders, we need to let people know that we won't stand by and let wasteful practices continue.

The best way to tackle this problem is with our people. They see waste much more intimately than we do. They're up close and personal with it. Enlist their help in killing that dragon.

CHAPTER 6 Banish Bureaucracy

"We are being ruined by the best efforts of people doing the wrong things."
—*W. Edwards Deming*

Thoughts

Many observers would argue that bureaucracy is the biggest enemy of most organizations. Alexis de Tocqueville, the prophetic observer of early America, believed that bureaucracy in both government and business would become the major problem facing this young democracy.

> "I am not, as I say, charging bureaucrats with inhumanity, malice, vindictiveness, or sadism. The vast majority are honest, efficient, hard-working: a great many of them are dedicated. That is precisely the problem of bureaucracy: the better it is, the worse its impact upon culture and social order. It is not the occasional evidence of venality or cruelty in the bureaucrat that makes one apprehensive. It is, rather, the much more common evidence of dispassionate, bland, emotionless fulfillment of job."
>
> *Robert Nisbet, author*

Bureaucracy is destructive to business because bureaucrats allow rules, procedures, policies, and routines to become the end objective. They lose sight of the purpose for which the job was created. They also lose sight of their larger responsibility to the customer or other internal associates as the bureaucratic mentality protects its small domain.

We use the term *bureaucracy* to describe organizations that:

1   Prefer formality in their structure and manner of operating.

2   Emphasize rules in place of reason. The rules are made by people high in the organization and enforced by people low in the organization. Exceptions to rules can be made only by people high in the organization.

3   Organize around functional specialties.

4   Focus upward and place the greatest emphasis on pleasing those to whom they report.

5   Treat those whom they serve impersonally.

I recall talking with the director of plant maintenance in a company I had just joined. I said, "If you had a call from the CEO asking that your crew come over and move some furniture in his office, and then you got a call reporting a serious water leak in the plant, which one would you respond to first?" Without hesitation he replied, "I'd go move the furniture." I tried over the months to change his priorities and his bureaucratic mindset, but I failed and he was terminated.

The defense of bureaucracy is that it protects the organization from the wide variances skill levels of employees. Limiting what any one person can do contains the damage one person could do to the institution and those it serves. But the cocoon we wrap around the individual to protect the organization becomes a numbing coffin that limits personal growth, robs employees of job satisfaction, and alienates them from those they serve.

Things to Do

1   Proclaim war on bureaucracy. Make sure everyone in your organization knows that you see it as an enemy. In the next chapter we suggest a way to tackle reports, approval processes, measures, policies, and practices that don't make sense. Those are some of the symptoms of the bureaucratic disease.

2   Set a target for reducing overhead and bureaucratic costs. Some companies have found that such costs run from 25 to 50 percent of their revenue dollars. Downsizing large corporate staffs is one way to do it, though it produces pain in the personal lives of those involved.

3   Make the pronoun "they" another enemy. Whenever some front-line person asks, "Why are we doing that?" you often hear, "Well, they want it done that way."

    Obliterate such language from the organization. Ask everyone's help in challenging anyone using that language. When someone says "they" want this, ask exactly who "they" are. If a decision doesn't make sense, go quickly to "them" and find out once and for all if "they" really want it. Assume that no one ever deliberately makes a dumb decision, so if a decision is being implemented that looks foolish to you, raise the issue.

4   Because bureaucracy thrives on rules, encourage everyone to challenge rules that don't make sense. Obviously, there are many good rules to follow. But everyone should be allowed to challenge a rule that is silly. (Such as the rule that you have to use deposit slips when making a deposit in a bank. They're unnecessary paper.)

5   Use technologies that diminish formal, rigid structures. Encourage the use of groupware, e-mail and ad hoc groups that work totally outside the hierarchical chain.

6   Encourage informality. I visited a British company. Hanging on the wall was a sign indicating what to do in case of a fire.

In the event of a fire breaking out, the senior most person in the room will ring up the fire department.

Reason might suggest that the person who is nearest a phone and sufficiently composed should call. But that sign is symptomatic of how bureaucratic thinking creeps into organizations.

7   Organize around processes. That totally upends traditional bureaucracy. It scatters people who have been clustered together in functional specialties and puts them into contact with others who are trying to serve customers better or make higher-quality products and to do it quicker.

8   Encourage everyone in the organization to focus outward, not upward. Let people know that serving customers comes before pleasing your boss. Serving customers should be what pleases the boss.

9   Push for broader spans of control. When leaders have more than 12 people to supervise, they can't micromanage them. The subordinates have to make decisions. They grow. Their commitment goes up.

10   Have people keep time logs of how they spend their hours in a day. Review these logs with them to see if you and they think those hours are well spent in those activities.

One company had 350 people working nearly full-time on budgets. Huge portions of other people's time was spent in preparing and modifying budgets and preparing detailed planning documents. Management decided that while it needed budgets, it could not justify that waste of time. So the process was drastically simplified.

11   Review the attitudes of staff people and their relationship to their line counterparts. I'm not against staff people. In fact, I think it's harder to find a really good staff executive than it is to find good line executives. The best staff people, however, see their job as being a resource for the line. They don't see themselves as cops. They see themselves as colleagues. Bureaucracy can be at its worst among corporate staff groups.

Tips & Afterthoughts

Keeping bureaucracy down, in my experience, requires two things to happen. One is a "daily housekeeping" activity in which you're always trying to hold the line on creeping bureaucracy. It involves not letting things get worse, not letting one more form get added or one more approval signature be required.

But fighting bureaucracy also requires "spring housecleaning" days where everyone gets together and says, "Let's look around and see where the house really needs a thorough cleaning." Everyone pitches in to beat back the encroaching bureaucracy.

Many managers can identify at least momentarily with the solution of one Soviet manager, Vladimir Karaidze, then general director of the Ivanovo Machine Building Works near Moscow. In a speech to the Communist Party Congress, he said: "I can't stand this proliferation of paperwork. It's useless to fight the forms; you've got to kill the people producing them."

I'm sure he was joking. At least, I hope he was joking.

CHAPTER 7 Start a Revolution

"We've got to force leaders who aren't walking the talk to face up to their people."

—Jack Welch, chairman of General Electric

Thoughts

The next step is a fun one. Do it and your organization will never be the same. It involves jump-starting the organization with a highly involving organization improvement process.

The most important thing to do when you begin a productivity improvement program is to get some points on the scoreboard. Get quick, tangible wins.

I was the CEO of a company that was among the early adopters of total quality management. We brought in as consultants people who had initiated the effort in one of the pioneering companies. The first step they proposed was to have everyone in the organization go through awareness training. So we brought everyone together and talked about quality, what it was, and what caused it to break down. We learned all the jargon of the total quality movement.

Guess what? Nothing happened! Awareness training did not do one thing to improve our quality. People got disenchanted. Most companies I know had to take at least two or three runs at quality before they got it moving, let alone getting it right. One reason for that was that they circled the topic endlessly instead of diving right to the heart of it.

Avoid that mistake. If you introduce a productivity improvement process, do it surefootedly. Focus on results, not activities. Speedily produce some results that are tangible to everyone.

The best example of this that I know is General Electric's WorkOut process. Much has been written about it, so I'm not going to go into great detail. (At the end of this chapter I'll tell you where to find more information.) First of all, what GE did was not fancy. The organization development gurus would describe it as a "plain vanilla" OD intervention. What was brilliant was the fact that Jack Welch institutionalized it. Large numbers of people participated. The impetus for this came from Welch, who believed that productivity had to grow twice as fast as it had been growing.

"One of the biggest planned efforts to alter people's behavior since Mao's Cultural Revolution."

Len Schlesinger, Harvard Business School professor, speaking about GE's Workout Process.

Because GE had taken people out of the system, Welch believed it needed to take "work" out of the system. His concept was to take unnecessary work out of GE through collaborative problem solving, done in a way that produced brightly visible, instantaneous results. He wanted realistic ideas for change.

The process GE implemented made it possible for everyone to streamline their work and jettison any nonsense they saw going on in the organization around them. It encouraged them to identify reports, procedures, policies, and approval steps that didn't make sense. It provided a forum for eliminating unnecessary activities and for people to present their recommendations directly to their senior executive, and get an on-the-spot decision. The few issues that needed more study had to be decided in less than one month.

That process electrified the organization. People saw that things could change as a result of their ideas. Not only was there no punishment for raising thorny issues, but upper management had given people the time, the resources, and lots of encouragement to come up with new recommendations. The frosting on the cake was that people at all levels discovered that the top manager agreed with their recommendations about 85 percent of the time.

In GE's terminology, they "picked a lot of low-hanging fruit." But who cared whether it was low-hanging or high on the tree? The fruit was delicious to the front-line workers who saw positive change happen.

In our work, day after day, we strive to solve problems and get our own work done. What we don't do is to step back and focus on how we could do our work better and better. We don't stop to think about ways to continually improve the way work gets done or how our group functions. We don't look at the breakdowns that occur at the junction boxes between our group and others. Individuals don't see how their work links to the rest of the organization. We seldom focus solely on how to improve the overall functioning of the enterprise. As a rule, people in organizations are not invited to give their ideas about how some other department could function more effectively, even though their distance often lets them see a sister department's problems more clearly than the people inside.

That's what WorkOut did.

Things to Do

You don't have to be an organization development consultant to ignite a revolution in your organization. Here's how you can do it.

1   Schedule a two-and-a-half day meeting with a selected group of your people. The group can range from 30 to 120 people. It's best to have a cross-section of people from different departments and different levels in the organization. Invite people to participate, but don't force them. Pretty soon, everyone will want to attend. Tell them you want to engage in an activity that is designed to make things better in your company. Call the event anything you

want—except WorkOut. While GE has been generous in describing its process, "WorkOut" is a proprietary name. So make up a name that fits your organization.

2   When possible, hold the first few meetings away from work. The locale doesn't need to be fancy, just someplace to get away from all the distractions of work. Once the process gets rolling, you can hold meetings on company premises.

3   Before the session, ask the participants to keep track of

   • Work that has to be repeated.

   • Approvals that don't add any value.

   • Reports that no one uses.

   • Policies that are covered with cobwebs and dust.

   • Practices that once made sense but no longer are reasonable.

   • Meetings that waste your time.

   • Things your boss asks you to do that don't make sense to you or seem like a waste of time.

   Ask participants to come to the meeting with notes on all those topics. Suggest that they focus on things that are largely under their control.

4   Kick off the meeting by telling people you are really interested in their ideas. Give everyone a sheet of chart-pad paper and a felt-tip marker. Ask them, "What one thing would you most like to see changed around here?" Give people a few minutes to write down their answers, big and legibly. Hang their answers up around the room with masking tape. Then tell the group that each person has five votes. You can give them stickers or tell them to go put a star on the five items that seem most important to them.

They proceed to walk around the room, read all of the sheets, and mark their five choices. Within a half-hour you'll begin to see a pattern emerge, and you can quickly select three to five topics for the group to tackle.

As an alternative, the managers in your organization may have some problems that they'd like groups to tackle. Again, these can be forms, approvals, reports, measures, policies, or any other serious topic. Present these to the group as topics management would like to see addressed, but leave it up to the group to decide whether to tackle those topics or others of their choosing.

5   Then divide the group into teams of four to seven people. Each team is to tackle one topic that got lots of votes. You'll decide how many topics to select based on the size of your total group. Each team should have its own unique topic to tackle. Have them analyze the problem; state why it is a problem, what will happen if it doesn't get resolved, and what the benefits of fixing it would be; and make their recommendations. Tell the group that the senior people will be back the afternoon of the third day to hear the team reports.

6   Have the senior executive who is responsible for this group come in on the last day to sit at the head of the room and hear presentations from each team. These presentations should be in the form or recommendations and action plans, not just rehearsals of problems or current conditions. They should be about 10 minutes long. At the end of each presentation, the senior executive can either say yes and sign a piece of paper acknowledging approval or say no and tell the group why. The executive can ask for more time but must provide a final answer within one month.

7   Follow up to make sure the agreements made in the session are implemented.

Tips & Afterthoughts

The consequences of this process are far-reaching. It galvanizes the organization. People see that they can influence decisions. They see that issues can get decided. They see that executives will listen to reason. That builds confidence in top management. I predict that you'll end up saying yes to about 85 percent of the recommendations. For many you'll be tempted to say, "Why haven't we been doing it that way all along?" I promise you, such a meeting will be a real eye-opener.

Schedule more sessions until you've included everyone who wants to participate. Follow that simple format, and you'll be amazed at the good ideas you'll get. Do it every few months. Let people know that you plan to repeat it in the future. Scraping barnacles off the hull of a ship is a neverending process.

Jump-starting the organization is the first step in a continuous improvement process. That's the message you want to get across. Future sessions will evolve into a new format or will focus on fresh topics. But this is a great beginning. The good news is that organizations can just keep getting better and better. There aren't any fetters or anchors holding you down. Growth and improvement opportunities are absolutely limitless.

Word will quickly get out if you do this well. The jungle drums will beat loud and clear and signal to everyone that you are serious about improvement. People will see that you want to do this *with* them, not *to* them. It's like taking the cap off a warm bottle of carbonated water that's been shaken up for several minutes. The ideas and enthusiasm come gushing out. Be prepared for a few skeptics and naysayers. But they'll be carried along by the rest of the group. Such people will always be with us; never let them deter you from doing the right thing.

Many organizations besides GE have embarked on similar programs. They've had universally great success. As time goes on, the kinds of problems you tackle can be more complex. The key is to get started.

Many companies talk about empowerment. The brilliance of GE's approach was that senior management didn't talk about it, they did something about it. They made simple, concrete, and practical changes. That's what's missing from most organizational improvement initiatives. They get fancy and theoretical and pay expensive consultants to swarm about. But often nothing practical or concrete happens.

If you don't feel competent to run such a session, hire a consultant to help you. But I'm convinced that most managers can make this work if they'll just try.

When you've involved all of your internal people in such sessions, start inviting in your suppliers and your customers. Kick off the session with your suppliers by asking them to tell you all of the dumb things you ask them to do. They'll gulp, but if you show you really want to hear, in time they'll tell you. One GE manager told me that they'd never failed to cut their costs with an outside supplier by at least 15 percent after going through a session like this.

With customers the format is nearly the same. Get a team of people from your organization and a team from theirs. Meet together and ask them to tell you what things you do that make their life more complicated and how the relationship could be structured to be of greater help to them.

Your company will never be the same after you do this. In the final analysis, most of us just want to make a difference. This process gives everyone that opportunity. Many will take it.

By the way, GE was able to improve its overall rate of productivity growth to 5 percent in 1990—more than double what it had been 10 years earlier.[3]

---

[3]Additional information about the GE WorkOut process can be found in:

Thomas A. Stewart, "GE Keeps Those Good Ideas Coming." *Fortune,* August 12, 1991, pp. 42–49.

Robert Slater, *Get Better or Get Beaten: 31 Leadership Secrets from GE's Jack Welch.* Burr Ridge, IL: Irwin Professional Publishing, 1994.

Noel Tichy and Stratford Sherman, "Walking the Talk at GE." *Training & Development Journal,* June 1993, pp. 28–34.

CHAPTER 8 Replant Deadwood

"Revolution is not a dinner party, nor an essay, nor a painting, nor a piece of embroidery; it cannot be advanced softly, gradually, carefully, considerately, respectfully, politely . . ."

—*Mao Tse-tung*

Thoughts

Nothing destroys the productivity and performance of a work group more than having some of the people not carrying their load, having everybody know it, and having management ignore the problem.

So the next action step is to deal effectively with poor performers.

When people don't succeed on a job, the reasons can be extremely complex. They may lack skill and fundamental competence. Or they may lack understanding about what is really expected of them, training, consequences for not performing, or rewards for performing well. They may feel pressures from their personal life, interpersonal friction with their co-workers—the list goes on.

Whatever the reasons, you simply cannot let poor performance go on.

But the main point is simple. Whatever the reasons, you simply cannot let poor performance go on. If you do, you will ultimately destroy the performance of the entire work group. They will resent your unwillingness to deal with poor performance, which they see so vividly and which drags down the performance of the group. Imagine the impact on a crew that was racing a scull if one rower just dangled the oars in the water, not keeping rhythm with the rest or putting forth any effort. You can be assured that the coach or the team would do something about it. Many work teams are carrying people exactly like that and waiting for management to act.

Things to Do

1   Assess the contributions of everyone who works in your group. Find fair ways of measuring performance. Measures of how people are performing differ from group to group because the work is so varied. In some team-based situations, it may be hard to identify who is not carrying a fair share of the load. Because few teams in today's organizations take the responsibility to terminate poor performers, the team will start dropping hints to you about what needs to be done.

   If you aren't in a team-based situation, then I'm assuming you have ways to track the objective and subjective goals of your people.

2   If you see someone's performance heading south, the worst thing to do is wait around and hope it will get better. Talk with them. Describe what you see happening calmly and objectively. But express your concern in a positive way. Ask if they understand why it is happening and jointly work out a plan of action to right the situation. Offer your help, of course.

   If you think you know why performance is dragging and the worker doesn't know, then you are in a classic coaching situation, where you can see things that the players just can't see in the thick of the game. Your responsibility is to give this person the benefit of your objective view and your experience. People development is a big part of your job. And it is one you can't delegate to anyone else.

Jointly work out a clear plan of action to fix the employee's performance. This must include a timetable with review dates. Do everything you can to help during this time. Make certain that you have follow-up discussions. If the person meets performance expectations, formally end the performance plan.

3   Every executive and manager I've known (and this absolutely applies to me), has often waited too long to get involved in solving performance problems. They're easier to fix when things aren't dreadful. They're terrible to fix when performance has plunged into the tank and been submerged for a long time.

4   Consult with the human resources department when you want to put someone on a performance plan, especially if you think it might end in termination. Given all the wrongful termination lawsuits and the huge costs involved in such litigation, it is mandatory to do everything according to the book.

5   If you can't get poor performers back on the right track, then don't just let things slide. You aren't doing them a favor. Getting them out is the best thing for them and for you. Often they end up in a much better situation. If you don't do something about it, everyone else in the organization will question whether you are a responsible leader. And if you don't do something about it, you aren't a responsible leader in my book.

6   When you terminate someone, don't go through a complete description of all shortcomings and foul-ups to justify what you are about to do. That's tempting because it is logical. But it is bad psychologic. It won't do any good at this time and has potential for great harm.

They'll never agree with you, so why try to convince them? Simply say in a calm voice that you've lost confidence in their ability to perform and have decided to terminate them from the company. Explain that you want to do this in the most constructive way possible and immediately begin to talk about when it will occur, the need to return any company property, when to turn over keys, and what any public announcement will say. Have their final check prepared and hand it to them. These steps signal that your mind is made up. There is no turning back. That usually forestalls any discussion of "I promise to change" or "Can't I have one more chance?" It is no longer a question of *if*; now it is a matter of *when* and *how*.

Tips & Afterthoughts

We often close our eyes to poor performance in two specific situations. One is when the employee has been there a long time. The other is when there is some reason to feel sorry for him or her. But in the long run, letting things slide is almost never a favor. If you don't fix the problem and you move on, your successor will have to do it, and it will be more difficult and more traumatic then. Further, it is not fair to your successor to have to clean up your mess. It's also not fair to the person involved to let more time pass.

You can remind this worker that people frequently move on from an organization where things weren't going all that well to one where they have wonderful success. Explain that the current position just wasn't a good match. If you were involved in the hiring decision, tell the employee you regret the mismatch and apologize for your part in it.

Above all, don't make it a long conversation. When a terminated employee leaves your office, he or she will usually go through a predictable cycle of shock, disbelief, self-pity, and anger. That may take a few days. When the person gets to the angry stage, they may reopen discussions on severance arrangements. But by that time the reality of the situation has set in.

Besides poor performance, there are other behaviors that warrant termination. David Ogilvy, the former chair of Ogilvy and Mather, wrote, "Sack incurable politicians." Others would urge you to terminate anyone who violates an ethical principle or whose values contradict those of your company.

These actions are the most disagreeable part of being a leader. Having to fire someone makes any decent human being feel rotten. But it's part of being a responsible leader.

This isn't the most pleasant of topics. I hope you don't have any poor performers in your group—but odds are that if you don't have one now, you will at some point. If you want to increase the productivity and performance of the whole group, deal with poor performers. Because termination often takes months to implement fully, start now to get things on the right track.

CHAPTER 9 Change Silos into Tunnels

"The typical large business 20 years hence
. . . will bear little resemblance to the
typical manufacturing company, circa 1950.
Traditional departments will serve as
guardians of standards, as centers for
training and the assignment of specialists;
they won't be where the work gets done."

—*Peter Drucker*

Thoughts

Much has been written and spoken about emphasizing work processes in contrast to conventional functional organizations. Everyone's heard of reengineering, and some have argued the differences between reengineering and work process improvement. Frankly, I don't think it's worth getting caught up in that debate. The scale of activities ranges from minor improvements in how a department handles paperwork all the way to a complete restructuring of how work gets done. Where one begins and the other leaves off is a fuzzy line.

The massive reengineering efforts have had mixed results, but one step that consistently brings solid benefit is to streamline work processes. Let's be sure we all know what that means. A work process is a flow of events and activities that are linked together to produce an end result. Often these components of the process are under the control of a functional department.

For example, when you apply for a mortgage loan, one department might complete the loan application papers, another analyze your creditworthiness, another appraise the real estate under consideration, and yet another draw up the loan documents and handle the escrow procedures. From the customer's point of view, this is all one process. From the lender's traditional point of view, these were different activities that required individual specialists who were each based in departments where they could be hired, trained, and supervised. The consequence was that when you applied for a loan, the entire process could take weeks as the paper flowed through this complex system.

Progressive lenders are now using an alternative organization structure. They create a team of people. Each has a specialty, but the team is assigned your application and is responsible for getting it out with no delays. The result is that some lenders are processing applications in hours instead of weeks.

When you organize around processes, you collapse levels of supervision and management. That opens the gate for many improvements. People doing the real work can now talk directly to each other. They see how their actions affect others and what changes can be made to accelerate the entire process. "Paper bombs" that used to get heaved over transoms at another department never get created.

Focusing on processes also allows problems to be resolved that have been festering for years. Invariably, when a problem plagues a firm like a fungus that won't go away, it is because it lives in the cracks between two departments. No one owns it. No one feels responsible for resolving it. So the problem lives quite comfortably in the underground crevices between departments, with many other wasteful problems just like it.

Problems between functional departments are magnified because these departments often have conflicting objectives. Purchasing wants to buy large quantities in order to get the best price. Finance wants to keep inventories low. Sales never wants to stock out but does want mass customization. Manufacturing wants long production runs of the same model for maximum efficiency.

Walk into any organization and you can wager that there are strains between those departments. That's not because they are cantankerous people or interpersonally inept. Most often it's because their predictable competing objectives are at odds with each other.

Processes change the measuring methods to reflect the best interests of the entire business, not any one department. What gives customers the greatest satisfaction? What reduces overall cycle time? What accelerates inventory turns? What increases the organization's productivity?

Process management also creates information systems that feed information to all interested parties simultaneously. That avoids any filtering as it passes through layers.

Things to Do

1   Define the three to six core processes that make up your business. Most organizations can build themselves around core processes, such as (1) researching market needs and developing new products, (2) designing and producing the products, (3) generating leads and making sales, (4) servicing and supporting customers, (5) receiving and fulfilling orders, and (6) invoicing and collecting money from clients. Work processes are the horizontal pipes cutting across an organization through which the work really flows. They are tunnels that replace the inefficient silos of a hierarchical organization.

2   Map how the work is occurring today. This process mapping can take the form of pins in a wall with yarn stretched between them to describe each step that occurs. It can be done with Post-it™ notes on a wall or a computer-generated diagram that describes work flows. Carefully document what is going on now. Involve the people in that department who actually do the work.

Begin with carefully analyzing *how* work is being done, not just measuring what is produced. You can keep all kinds of detailed records on how much is produced, but you'll never know why productivity is high or low until you carefully lay out how work is accomplished upstream.

You can watch the product come off the assembly line and head for order fulfillment. You can make all kinds of measurements at that point regarding quality, cost, and time to produce it. But you'll never be able to make any reasonable improvements until you track the product all the way upstream to see what happened to it along the way. That tracking of how work gets done is work process analysis.

When you take the time to document each step, you will suddenly become aware of all of the redundancies, the bottlenecks, and places where inadequate resources exist. You'll be able to figure out why delays are occurring.

3   Organize around those strategic processes and their subprocesses. It is far better to have one team performing several steps on one process than to have several departments each performing one step. Appoint a manager of the process and hold that person's feet to the fire regarding how well the process works.

Many companies are organizing themselves around processes, eliminating such traditional departments as sales, marketing, accounting, finance, engineering, production control, quality assurance, and customer service. Multidisciplinary teams carry out most of the work, so the organization has fewer layers. This profound change transforms the culture.

This structure also simplifies the way things get done. With fewer connections in the organization structure, less energy is wasted.

Imagine a track team where each runner carries the baton 30 yards and then puts it in an in basket for the next team to pick up at its leisure. Then a person from team #2 runs 30 yards and puts the baton in another box, awaiting team #3's decision to come and get it. Each team is rewarded for moving batons 30 yards, but they can decide to wait for five batons to accumulate and take them all at once if they choose. That describes a traditional functional organization.

4   Once the analysis of how things are being done now has been accomplished, then comes the fun of deciding how to improve it. The greatest success usually comes from tipping the organization on its side and organizing around horizontal work processes.

"We investigated why in-hospital patients were arriving late for CT scans, thereby leaving this very expensive piece of equipment sitting idle. So we called together the four groups of people involved: the CT technicians, the secretaries in radiology who called for the patients, the transporters who brought the patients down, and the nurses who got them ready on their patient care units. At the meeting, each group had already prepared a document as to why it was not their fault.

To deal with the problem, we worked with these four groups together to develop a flow chart of the processes that were taking place. We thereby discovered that each group had a different definition of "on time."

Not only was a new process developed which reduced the average wait from 15 minutes to less than five minutes, but the socialization of those four groups turned them into a team."

Mitchell T. Rabkin, president of Boston's Beth Israel Hospital, in The Conference Board's Report #1039, Productivity: Key to World Competitiveness, 1993.

Tips & Afterthoughts

Efficiency comes when the organization manages the spaces in between the functional departments or decides to eliminate some of those spaces all together.

The fundamental question of work process redesign is simple: "If we didn't have anything in place and we were starting from scratch, how would we do this?" Do your best to come as close to that ideal work process as possible. This takes time and perseverance. Analyzing a work process and then redesigning it is not glamorous. It's more like slogging through eight inches of mud for three miles while carrying a heavy backpack. But dumping silly work is highly rewarding.

Once the work has been done, the outcomes can be spectacular. Many companies have saved huge amounts of money and time. If you studied the top 20 organizations as measured by their annual improvement in productivity, you would find that they have spent a great deal of time and money streamlining their work processes. Indeed, they are usually organized around these processes, rather than in the more traditional functional manner.

Changing silos into tunnels needs your support. You can't delegate it. Help select the strategic processes that hurt customers or cut away at your firm's ability to compete.

Improving work processes can be done two ways:

1   Make large, dramatic improvements.

2   Generate a host of tiny improvements.

It's the combination of these two that makes the firm operate more effectively. We've debated in the past which of these two was the right approach. We desperately need them both.

Many organizations have specialists who work with teams to help them analyze and streamline their work processes. They consistently get 30 to 50 percent improvement in performance if the group is willing to abandon traditional ways of doing things and implement a redesigned process. This is a huge, time-consuming task. But I promise that the payoffs are worth the effort you'll spend to make it happen.

CHAPTER 10 **Play Squash**

"Growth for the sake of growth is the idealogy of the cancer cell."
—*Edward Abbey*

Thoughts

The next action step for producing more with less involves finding ways to flatten the organization structure.

No one will ever know how our business and government organizations became so bloated. We added people because we thought they would increase our overall productivity and performance. They didn't. Often people got added because having a big department was the way managers increased their personal importance and compensation. We added people when we lacked the discipline to fix cumbersome or broken work processes. We added people because bigger seemed better. Throwing more people onto a task created the illusion that progress was being made. The task ultimately got accomplished, but often despite the number of people involved, not because of them.

We built larger and steeper pyramids than the pharaohs ever contemplated. But through all those years of adding people and building "wedding-cake"[4] organizations, there was clear evidence that it was a mistake. In the 1940s a researcher working inside

---

[4]One wag observed that the wedding-cake organization consists of multiple layers of successively smaller size, with well-dressed people in formal attire dancing at the top.

Sears compared the performance of stores that had multiple layers to those that were flatter. Flatter always performed better. Those flat stores were more nimble in responding to their markets, and they attracted different managerial talent. Flat-structured stores were a magnet for aggressive, risk-taking entrepreneurial people. Organizations that looked like an Alpine skiing cabin attracted more cautious, bureaucratic people, who liked the security of having layers of approval and not being held accountable for anything.

My experience is that often our highest quality and greatest efficiency most often come from plants with fewer than 200 employees. Bigger plants can be efficient, but there is some magic about people knowing their co-workers and feeling part of a compact organization. Bigger is rarely better.

The lesson has been a painful one to learn. In the 1980s, approximately 4 million people lost jobs in large organizations as they downsized. In this decade, 300,000 people have been removed from our Fortune 100 companies. Since 1992, IBM has announced staff reductions of 122,000 people. AT&T has cut 83,000 (and announced in early 1996 their intent to remove another 40,000). GM has laid off 74,000 people and Sears 50,000. To the degree that those laid off leave unproductive jobs and move into work that is more productive, both the economy and the firms are better off. Unfortunately, the individuals often aren't.

As you look at your own organization, roughly calculate your "tooth-to-tail" ratio. How many people are engaged in actually producing your product or serving your customers? What's the ratio of administrative and support staff to those doing "real work"?

A hotel chain executive told me that in its Southern California division, 148 people were checking the checkers, who in turn checked the work of the housekeepers in the hotels.

Things to Do

Your task is to look hard at your current structure.

1   Are the levels really necessary? What are they adding? If an entire level were removed, could the organization continue to function well? Once some of our largest corporations had more than 30 layers of management. Others seemed to function well with only seven or eight layers (with a comparable number of people).

2   Could the number of people reporting to every business leader be increased? It used to be an axiom of management that one person's span of control should be seven to 12 people. That principle was chiseled into the granite foundation of Fortune 500 organizations and under the ivy on the business school buildings. Then some companies began to experiment with much larger spans of control. One leader might have as many as 50 people reporting to him or her. Teams became more common, and self-directed work teams performed effectively with no immediate supervisor or manager controlling them.

3   Can people become more self-managing? Can several teams report to one leader, with the team taking on many of the duties and activities that were previously a manager's?

4   Will a revamping of the work processes allow for the same amount of work to be done with fewer people? If that is a possibility (and it almost always is), then begin immediately to change the work processes as discussed in Chapter 9.

Tips & Afterthoughts

A major benefit of a flatter organization structure is that it creates an environment in which people become more productive. That's because they are better informed. They have more interaction with the business leaders. They have more responsibility, which generates more commitment. There are fewer layers to filter information. People interact directly with each other rather than counting on a supervisor or manager to be the intermediary. Front-line people are more apt to connect with customers. Jobs broaden in scope, giving people more skills and knowledge.

Every key activity and function necessary to make a business succeed works better in a flatter organization. Communication speeds up. Decisions are made with better information and more rapidly. People's understanding of the organization is enhanced. Layers of approval are reduced, making for speedier decisions. Paperwork is slashed.

The biggest downside of a flatter organization used to be the reduction in promotional opportunities. But the days of defining career success by promotions are ending. Instead, career success is increasingly measured by what people are learning, the significance of the projects on which they work, and the in-depth expertise they gain in a specific discipline. Lifelong careers inside one organization are becoming rare.

If some people become unnecessary in the new structure, don't forget that those who remain judge the enterprise by how it treats those who are terminated. Do everything possible to prepare them for careers in the new world. Provide generous severance packages. Treat them with care and dignity. And pay lots of attention to those who are left behind. They feel a sense of loss and often betrayal. They are grieving for friends lost. When executives acknowledge the pain they personally are feeling, it often helps everyone to deal with downsizing.

That's the next step toward productivity. It raises a number of difficult issues, especially if some people are no longer needed. You owe it to those who leave to help prepare them for new work assignments.

Part 3

Raise the Bar

"I've met a few people in my time who were enthusiastic about hard work. And it was just my luck that all of them were men I happened to be working for at the time."

Bill Gold

The following six chapters describe what the leader does to raise people's sights—to elevate the bar. Chapter 11 describes a way to significantly raise people's sights through the use of benchmarking. Chapter 12 touts the virtues of speed and the importance of reducing cycle times for everything you do (in contrast to the current focus in most organizations on merely reducing cost). Chapter 13 deals with hiring and assimilation of new employees. One sure way of raising the bar is to improve the quality of the people we hire.

Chapter 14 provides a simple yet sure-fire recipe for increasing productivity: Identify your best performers and teach others to perform the way they do. Chapter 15 describes the benefits of outsourcing. This ultimate form of benchmarking simply suggests that if you're doing something that isn't one of your core competencies, and you can find someone else who does it cheaper and faster and meets your quality standards, seriously consider outsourcing the task. Chapter 16 shows you how to coach your people to better performance.

CHAPTER 11 Get on the Gold (Medal) Standard

"Know your enemy and know yourself, and in a hundred battles you will never be in peril."

—*Sun Tzu, The Art of War*

Thoughts

The next action step I'm proposing is one of the most powerful techniques of recent years. It involves benchmarking against the best.

Benchmarking involves measuring yourself against the highest-performing organizations that you can find. It compares your products, services, and practices against those of world-class competitors. The basic premise is easy. It's against the law of averages to assume that any one company is going to be best in everything. (Yes, I know that some loyal people think theirs is, but it's just not true.) So benchmarking, and its cousin, "best practices," are ways to make comparisons with the best.

In a nutshell, each group looks around to find the best "whatever you are" that exists. So whether you manage a human resources department or a manufacturing group, find the best one of those that you can, and work out a way to find out as much as you can about what that high-performing group does that makes it so effective. The challenge is to bring those best practices back into your organization. But you don't want merely to copy them; you want to make them even better. More about how to do that in a moment.

This approach is similar to finding the best performer in any work group and training the other front-line people to function like that top performer. (See Chapter 14, Clone Your Stars.) In this case, you're just going outside your own company to look throughout your industry, or in any industry anywhere in the world, for the best performers.

First, let me explain why this is so significant. It is a powerful device to help you and all the people around you overcome arrogance and complacency, twin demons that beset all managers. You get a stiff dose of humility when you see smart, progressive organizations functioning much better than you.

Benchmarking is powerful because it is so specific. It presses your nose up against hard data. Many managers and executives are like runners in a race who have their eyes closed. They know they're running hard and assume they're way out in front. Benchmarking opens your eyes and reveals that not only are you *not* out in front—you're way behind the pack. When you involve your people in visiting other organizations and collecting data, they can see for themselves that others have figured out ingenious ways to make huge improvements in work processes. There's an incentive to become more productive.

It's hard to drive change from the top down. People resist when you breeze in and tell them how to do their jobs differently. But when they go out and see someone performing a function very much like theirs in one-fifth the time, more accurately, and more cheaply, then you don't have to make condescending speeches. When your people get out and see firsthand what's happening, they'll also see things that executives would never pick up. They'll notice subtle things other companies do that make a big difference. Executives tend to miss those nuances because they're not close enough to the action.

Twenty-five Fortune 500 firms compared their data on several financial functions, including the cost of handling payroll checks. The average cost per check for the entire group was $6. If your company's cost

was $4 or $5, you'd feel pretty smug—until you discovered that the best company in the study was processing checks for 72 cents each.

That same thing held true for travel and entertainment reimbursements, accounts payable, and accounts receivable. The best was in some cases one-tenth of the average.

What to benchmark? Products, services, work processes, organization structure, strategies, staffing levels—the list is endless.

Who to benchmark against? They can be other internal departments, other organizations in your same industry, or organizations with some totally different function. In some early stories of benchmarking, Xerox compared its shipping and delivery with those of Domino's Pizza and L. L. Bean. (That was a real eye-opener.)

Things to Do

1   Decide what you want to benchmark. That choice is often driven by where you feel pain. Or it could be where you intuitively know that big improvements are tantalizingly close.

2   Plan the way you'll go about it. Who should you see? What questions do you want to ask? What data would be most helpful to collect?

3   Agree on the measurements you will use. Presumably a team of people will visit the other company. Get their help in deciding what data to collect and which measurements to use.

4   Carefully study your existing process so you can share it with the organization you'll visit. Be ready to compare your process with theirs. Benchmarking works best as a two-way street.

5   Find the best organizations through some active research that includes industry experts, consultants, professors, trade publications, or general business publications.

6   Make the visit and collect the information you've agreed is important. If possible, share your data with your host organization.

7   After analyzing the data you've gathered, present your recommendations for change to upper management (where necessary). Make the changes under your control as soon as possible.

Tips & Afterthoughts

One word of caution. If you're a beginning tennis player, the best person to watch is probably a good intermediate player, not Pete Sampras. If your group is doing something badly, don't study the world-class example. That would just demoralize your people. One study showed that when low-performing organizations compared themselves to the best in sales and marketing, there were some negative effects.

Again, the beauty of benchmarking is that it shoves people out of their rut. You see how organizations are going about doing something totally differently from the way you do it.

Mazda had five people in accounts payable while Ford had 500. Even allowing for volume differences, Ford had at least five times as many people as Mazda performing that function. What was different was not how hard people were working. Ford was performing a great number of activities, including matching up invoices with purchase orders and receipts and carefully

recording returns and allowances. Mazda was using a virtually paperless system in which it elected not to worry about all that; it simply tracked the factory output and paid suppliers for their part of each car that was shipped.

A variation on benchmarking involves identifying organizations that display superior overall performance and then figuring out what accounts for that superlative performance. That's what GE called its "best practices" study. It identified 25 companies that for 10 years had sustained higher productivity growth than GE had. (Note that productivity was the key criterion for choosing companies to study.) GE then analyzed the management practices in those firms and based many of its changes on them.

One last thing. Years ago Hal Leavitt, a Stanford business school professor and a friend of mine, said, "The most valuable time you'll ever spend as a manager or executive is the time *out* of your office." At the time I thought he was nuts, but I've come to agree with him. Nothing beats getting away from your own operation and seeing how someone else is doing it.

Don't forget that the better you get, the more value benchmarking has to you. The highest-performing companies consistently benefit the most.

CHAPTER 12 Watch the Clock

"Less than 5 percent of the total time required to manufacture and deliver a product is spent on actual work."

—*John D. Blackburn, Vanderbilt University*

Thoughts

Productivity has several basic components. One is obviously the quantity of goods and services produced. Another is the time required to produce them, and still another is the amount of inputs required.

Let's take the example of a company that makes complex machinery. For the sake of discussion, assume that the plant produces five machines in five weeks. If it suddenly begins to produce twice as much output in the same time, say 10 machines in five weeks (using the same labor force), it has doubled productivity. But if the company produces five machines in two-and-one-half weeks, that's even better. The company has compressed the overall cycle time of producing machines, and that has some distinct additional advantages.

When you produce the same amount in half the time, costs go down. Cascading from that are a host of other benefits.

- Market share increases because customers prefer your quick response time. The quick-lube shops for cars are one example. Others are convenience outlets, fast-food operations, and Land's End, FedEx—or any organization for which speed is a competitive advantage.

- Financial results improve because fewer assets are tied up in raw materials, inventory, or work in process.

- Premium prices can often be charged for speed. This has been a long tradition for dry cleaners and other service companies. FedEx can charge premium prices for speedy package and letter delivery.

"There are three sources of advantage, whether in commerce, war, or politics: quickness, strength, and morale."

Sun Tzu, The Art of War

Things to Do

1   Find out from your customers where time is important to them. Once an order is placed, your clock is ticking. Until then, it's their clock ticking, but their slow pace doesn't reduce your need for speed in fulfilling their wishes.

2   Partner with customers, using time and speed to cement the relationship. Like sole-source suppliers in the automotive industry, you can completely capture a client.

3   As you streamline work processes, make cycle time reduction, not merely cost savings, a key objective. In fact, shift from a cost mentality to a time mentality in your accounting and reporting.

4   Train front-line employees to perform up to the standards of your fastest people. Benchmark outside organizations, using speed as a selection criterion.

5   Use technology that helps work move faster. Computer-aided design and manufacturing (CAD-CAM) does this for manufacturing. Sales force automation (contact management,

opportunity management, marketing encyclopedias, and proposal writers) shows great promise for speeding up the sales and marketing functions. New information technologies can help many administrative functions. Sophisticated new techniques in marketing research speed information to make corrections in marketing programs.

6   Remember that 80 percent of new products fail. So change your product development mentality from one of doing vast research in hope of getting the product right the first time to one that includes

- trying more experiments.

- reducing the time it takes to get to success or failure.

- curtailing the cost of failures.

- maximizing what you learn from every experiment.

7   Aim to be the first to market. In general, the company that is first gets half of the market. The second does well to get 25 percent market share, and the latecomers divide the rest.

8   Set lofty goals for new-product introductions. One auto company has achieved a one-year cycle time from model to production, compared to Detroit's standard five years. Yet back in 1955, Chevrolet reduced the time to launch one new car to two years. (Miraculously, that was in the days before computers.)

"The way leading companies manage time—in production, new-product development and introduction, sales and distribution—represents the most powerful new sources of competitive advantage."

George Stalk, Jr., Boston Consulting Group

Tips & Afterthoughts

You'll see that many of the action steps are now beginning to fit together. Speed links to both understanding customers' expectations and improved work processes. Many of the suggestions that came out of your organization improvement process probably had to do with increasing speed.

Research confirms that companies improve productivity when they integrate a number of improvement activities. Changing one thing by itself isn't going to help much. But if you put several actions together, you'll be amazed by their power. No one ingredient, however tasty, creates a complete meal. Changing only one thing in an organization presupposes that there was only one problem or one opportunity. That's seldom the case.

I can't emphasize enough the importance of moving and acting versus perpetually studying things. There will always be people who want more data, want more time, want to hire a consultant to study the problem, and want to talk to more people. They're well intentioned. They're also scared.

We've created the illusion that a good executive is right nearly all the time. The truth is, we're all human; if we can make more right decisions than wrong ones and minimize the cost of the bad ones, we'll do just fine. Even all-star baseball players rarely hit more than .300.

Speed is universally relevant. For example, when President George Bush chose John Sununu to be his chief of staff, the irascible Sununu was generally not liked by the White House staffers. He said to one of them: "Why is it that everyone who meets me takes an instant dislike to me?"

Without hesitation, the young staffer replied, "It just saves time, I guess."

CHAPTER 13 Keep Diamonds in the Rough

"The closest to perfection a person ever comes is when he fills out a job application form."

—Stanley J. Randall

Thoughts

The next action step is to find ways to strengthen your hiring and assimilation process. You probably have a human resources department and procedures for recruiting and hiring people. Maximize these valuable resources to help you find the most productive employees available.

Hire the Best People

In Chapter 1 there is a summary of the enormous differences in the productivity of people. (Top software programmers are 16 times as productive as the least productive ones. For people in medium-complexity jobs, such as engineers, chemists, or craftspeople, the top performers are nearly twice as productive as the average ones.) We don't pay enough attention to finding star performers.

Southwest Airlines hires selectively. In one year, from 90,000 applicants it hired 1,000 people. It carefully selects people who are service oriented and who thrive on being part of the team effort that is so vital to Southwest's method of operation.

One painful lesson that human resources professionals have learned through the years is to take cautiously what people say about themselves in hiring interviews. While nearly always well-intentioned and honest, people often lack self-awareness.

Instead, look at what they've done in the past. That's the overwhelming predictor of what they'll do in the future. Look for indications of real accomplishment in *anything:* sports, art, student government, starting a club or a small business as a kid.

Look for achievement and a pattern of high productivity. While you can nurture it, hiring someone who is achievement oriented is much easier than trying to force-feed that mentality. Also look for signs that the person is a team player. Our organizations today work best with team players. There are few billets left for the loner.

Human resources people can help you spot those qualities if you just make it clear to them what you're after. It is fashionable in some circles to demean the role of human resources. Don't fall into that trap. Involve them in your strategic plans and the day-to-day tactics. Make them partners in finding and developing the people you need to make your group succeed. HR is supplying your most valuable raw material—the people who make up the company and your work team.

The skills, intelligence, and work ethic that people bring to their job give them a head start on getting to high levels of productivity. Their capacity sets the ultimate boundaries for their achievements.

Emphasize Thorough Assimilation

When people make the transition from school to work, or from one job to another, you've got them at one of the most malleable times in their life. They are willing to learn. They've left a comfort zone of predictability to try something new. Their life is turbulent. It is the perfect time to shape them to fit into your organization.

So what do most companies do? They herd new people into a room where someone from HR reviews the medical and dental plan and they sign the forms for insurance benefits. The HR person gives them a 20-minute presentation on the history of the company and sends them back out on the job. What a colossal waste!

They've missed the best opportunity to build loyalty. Worse yet, they've blown a big opportunity to help new people become productive quickly. You can significantly reduce turnover and help people get to peak productivity with a thorough assimilation and orientation process. I'm talking about a series of events that takes six months and involves you as their leader, upper management, HR, and the new employee.

Things to Do

1   Set rigorous specifications for people you hire. Use your best performers as the template. Get suggestions from people who are doing that job now for the qualities to seek and for suggestions regarding potential hires. People referred by current employees nearly always are a better fit and stay longer. (Maybe that's because they already have one good friend inside the organization.)

2   Screen many applicants to find the best. I know it's time-consuming. You want someone right now and it is tempting to accuse HR of dragging its feet. But don't cave in. Never compromise on the quality of people you hire. Calculate their salary and benefits over the next five years. Then consider the amount of management scrutiny that would be given a piece of capital equipment for that same cost.

3 Involve HR in finding people with the traits you seek. Include the traits that relate to high productivity, attentiveness to customers, and willingness to be a team player.

4 Don't rely solely on interviews. The time spent in reference checks, psychological testing, and a review of the applicant's past work output pays off a great deal more than interviews.

5 Have new employees accept some of the responsibility for their own assimilation. They need to tell their manager the things they need to know, people they need to meet, or skills they need to acquire. This can't be something we do *to* people. It must become something we do *with* them.

6 Familiarize new employees with the vast array of resources available, ranging from experts inside the organization, manuals, training classes, and help from outside resources.

7 Provide diagnostic procedures to let new hires know how much they need to learn or how their current skill level compares with what you expect. Everyone needs a benchmark.

8 Assign a senior employee as a "buddy" for each new employee. That senior person should be coached to let the new hire know that the organization has high standards but that you are all convinced he or she will do well. Assure new employees that there is a high success rate in your company. But right from the beginning show them how you measure their performance and how their productivity matches up to your expectations.

9 Make new employees feel that they're among friends. Starting in a new organization is a time of anxiety. Ask each senior buddy to find out what the new person is expecting from the job. Then meet those expectations wherever possible.

10 Make new employees feel productive as early as possible. Nothing is worse than standing around for weeks watching others work. Give people assignments that make them feel highly productive and let them hit the ground running.

11   Don't give new employees a huge data dump on their first day at work. Give them information in small doses. The assimilation process will probably take about six months. Don't try to cram it all into the first day.

12   Make the assimilation process a well orchestrated series of activities by the HR department, other executives, yourself, the new person's team members and the new person. There is usually an enormous amount of information to acquire, and the more rapidly new employees get it, the more productive they'll be and the fewer mistakes they'll make. Information about fringe benefits is actually the least important in the first months. Far more important is workers' thorough understanding of your business, your customers, the financial performance of the company, how they get the resources they need, where they can turn for help, and how they'll be evaluated.

Tips & Afterthoughts

The challenge is how fast you can move people from feeling like "hired hands" to feeling like "owners."

Separate the company orientation from the department or team orientation. Each has different things to cover.

An investment in getting people knowledgeable and truly acculturated to their new organization pays incredible dividends. First, you get their flow of productivity early on. Second, turnover is a killer for most companies. When top performers walk out the door, they're taking valuable knowledge and experience plus a huge investment with them. But the worst thing is that they're taking away a stream of productivity that is hard to replace.

Getting the long-term front-line people involved in assimilating new hires keeps them tuned into the changes the organization is going through. You need the the old-timers to stay up to speed with the organization. This new employee orientation refreshes the entire organization.

CHAPTER 14 Clone Your Stars

"One of the best ways to raise productivity is to look for your top performers and put them to teaching others. When they teach, it forces them to think through what they are doing and to systematically present it. It also convinces them to use successful methods and to take what they are doing seriously. Use your performers; if they raise their own performance, the performance of the whole group will go up."

—*Peter Drucker*

Thoughts

People live up to what's expected of them. Whether it is school-children, new employees, or Eliza Doolittle, there is a Pygmalion effect. People's behavior is influenced by the expectations of others.

So how does a leader communicate to everyone in the group that a great deal is expected of them? And even more difficult, how do you do it in a constructive way that preserves their self-esteem?

Consider again the table in Chapter 1 that describes the huge differences in productivity between the top and bottom performers. What would your organization be like if one-third of your people performed like your top person? If we hold the star up as an example, we've clearly set a lofty expectation. If we go further and teach a major portion (20 to 30 percent) of our front-line people to pattern their behavior after the top 1 percent, imagine the consequences. We've let everyone know that we're serious about high productivity and that it is recognized and appreciated.

Managers ought to familiarize themselves with the jobs they supervise. That doesn't mean they need to be experts or do the job better than anyone else. That's unreasonable. But they should understand of what their people do. It doesn't hurt anybody to go out and work in the plant for a week. Disney executives periodically go out to their theme parks and load guests onto rides. The top people of AES, go work in power plants loading coal into boilers.

"Every manager at ServiceMaster spends training time actually doing the task that he or she will ultimately manage and lead others to do. It is this hands-on involvement that helps us focus, for example, on the importance of the tools of production in assisting the service provider to be more productive."

C. William Pollard, chairman of ServiceMaster Corp.

Things to Do

1   Identify your stars. This sounds disarmingly easy, but it isn't. In many organizations I've encountered, it was impossible to get any agreement on who the best performers were. But through a combination of managerial nominations and peer selection, you can usually find the people whose outputs best meet the company objectives. You need only one or two stars.

2   Find out what the stars do differently. Begin by looking at how their outputs differ from others. Then look at

the subelements of each output. See if you can discern differences in the way they reach their outputs. How do they go about their work differently from the average worker?

For example, the best salespeople often prospect differently. They spend one day in the office to set up appointments and finish paperwork, and then they're in the field for four active days. They often don't make cold calls, but insist on having appointments to see all prospects or customers. Those differences would appear to account for much of their superior sales performance.

3 Don't rely on top performers to tell you what makes them good. They often don't know! It's intuitive to them. They assume everyone thinks like they do. And even when they do know, they may not be able to articulate the reasons.

4 Finally, find out what information the high performers possess that may be different from what the average performer knows. What were they thinking about when they were doing their work? You have to be a sleuth to discover what sets them apart from the average.

5 Enlist the stars' help in teaching others, especially new people. You can anticipate several reactions, so be prepared. They'll be flattered. But they'll also be nervous because often they don't know what makes them successful. They'll be afraid you're going to discover that their secret is trivial and "they'll be exposed." Best performers are often insecure people who have spent their lives proving that they're valuable by producing at high levels. That's how they reassure themselves that they're OK.

Some are reluctant to share their secrets because then they won't be special and get attention from management. Worse yet, they fear that if more people perform at their level, their compensation may be cut back. So be prepared for some confusing reactions when you ask people to share their success secrets.

6   Develop some reward system to assure your stars that there won't be any negative consequences for sharing their discoveries.

7   Have your training staff help the top performers develop the best ways to teach others what they do. Generally speaking, the best learning is highly active. People need to actually try the new methods and have the top performer observe what they do. That peak performer can often tell when something is being done wrong and coach them on how to do it better, even if he or she had a hard time articulating the skill in the first place. Most of us are better coaches of concrete behaviors than abstract theories.

Tips & Afterthoughts

Be certain to find some reward mechanisms for those top performers who share their techniques. It's hard to overestimate their value to your group if you can get more people to perform like they do. Prove to them that they made a good decision when they taught others how to perform to their standards.

People who aren't top performers often attribute the success of high producers to their political skills or other red herrings. They're often amazed when they discover what really accounts for the top performer's success. (Success is just a matter of luck; ask any person who is failing.)

Expect great results. Bell Labs created a class for average performers to learn to perform like the best. Over 600 engineers participated in a six-week course. Participants reported productivity gains of 20 percent after the end of the program and 25 percent a year later. Managers of the participants rated them twice as productive as nonparticipants in behaviors such as identifying and solving problems, finishing work on time, satisfying customers, keeping their manager informed, working effectively with other departments, understanding the competition, and supporting management decisions.

CHAPTER 15 Join 'em if You Can't Beat 'em

"Claims that we have given away the core . . . are untrue. We have given away things that were not good in order to accelerate and liberate the core.

. . . recognize that as long as there are aligned strategic goals, the long-term benefits will be profound."

—Jim Maxmin, CEO, Laura Ashley, Plc

Thoughts

No firm can do everything at the peak. There just isn't enough energy and time to be world class in every category of a business operation. There aren't many athletes who make the Olympics in more than one sport, and I don't know of many companies that excel in more than two or three core competencies. So if you can't be the best, find someone who is. Partner with them and you both win. That's the beauty of outsourcing.

Outsourcing is the ultimate approach to benchmarking. It takes your current performance and compares it to those top-flight suppliers on the outside.

If something isn't your core competency, let go of it. Let others do it if they are better, faster, or cheaper than you are. Chances are your management group is spending one-third to two-thirds of its time on issues that aren't your core competencies. You're driving yourselves nuts and losing sleep about activities that aren't your core skills. Worse yet, even if you get them perfectly right, chances are they won't be the areas that will propel you to market leadership. Unfortunately, the converse isn't true. If you don't get them right, your competitors will eat your lunch (and your dinner).

Outsourcing isn't exactly a new idea. Anything companies buy from others can be considered outsourcing. That ranges from raw materials to office supplies to legal services.

The history of outsourcing is instructive. It began with companies contracting for janitorial services, security, and food services. In most cases they had been doing those activities with their own employees but decided others could supply the people and better manage those functions. Those activities were peripheral to the mainstream business. They were safe. Then companies began to outsource payroll and data processing—activities closer to home. That also worked well.

Now we're seeing every function come under scrutiny. Accounts payable, accounts receivable, asset management and human resources functions. (We've outsourced pension and benefits administration in the past, but I'm talking about recruiting, hiring, training and development, and other traditional HR functions.) Many manufacturing activities have been outsourced to component suppliers. In fact, many so-called manufacturers are really assemblers.

We're seeing sales and marketing functions outsourced. VARS (value-added resellers) are important channels for countless companies. Telesales and telemarketing are often turned over to specialized outside firms. Order fulfillment is increasingly being handled by companies with state-of-the-art equipment and systems.

Many organizations have cut costs 30 to 40 percent by outsourcing. Better yet, the outside vendors are more productive, because they'll work harder to reengineer work processes, acquire the best technology, and bring sophistication to the management that a nonspecialized firm would never have.

However, there may be reasons beyond cost and quality for keeping a function in-house. An activity may require an exceptional level of expertise and training that you don't want to divulge to an outside firm. (This is really saying you can't find an outside supplier you can trust.) Or the activity may be so mission critical that you wouldn't ever want to be beholden to outside firms to provide it. Or your liaison with the outsourcing firm may be too complicated and time-consuming. I don't want to make this sound like an easy decision. It isn't.

Things to Do

1 Define your core competencies. Be totally honest about what you are and are not good at. What really distinguishes you from your competitors, or from other companies within your industry? Select a few truly defining characteristics.

2 Find outside suppliers to be potential outsourcers for the noncore activities that eat up management time and attention. Compare their costs with your own. If you find a supplier whose times, costs, service levels, and quality are satisfactory (and you trust it and can manage it), then proceed to the next steps.

3 Carefully choose an outsource partner with which to work. Select it on the basis of shared vision and values, not merely on a price quote.

4 Gain agreement on the overall strategy. Have the outsourcer lay out the steps it will take as it assumes this activity. It's important that you fully buy into your partner's strategy.

5 Let the outsource partner reengineer the process. It should decide all matters of implementation. Your only concern is the end result and how it touches the customer. Never meddle in the outsourcer's internal operation.

6   Tie the outsourcer's rewards and compensation to measures
that clearly line up with your goals.

Tips & Afterthoughts

One concern of most companies considering outsourcing is the
loss of control. But as long as contracts with your outsourcing
company are clear and specific and you have included important
measures of job performance, there is no reason to feel that
you've lost control of an important function.

Another issue is security. How dangerous is it to reveal to an
outside firm your financial data, customer lists, and cost
structures? Those were the same concerns companies expressed
when they considered having service bureaus handle data
processing. Those security concerns were easily allayed.

Acknowledging that another firm can do things better than
we're doing them is a difficult psychological hurdle. We all like
to think we're good and our people competent. It's hard to
remember that if someone else performs a function better than
we can, everyone wins when the more competent specialist
handles the function.

Finally, don't procrastinate. It's easy to go back and forth,
agonizing over these decisions. Once you've determined that the
outside firm can do it to your standards and at a better price,
don't delay.

CHAPTER 16 Coach Extensively

"Where no counsel is, the people fail: but in the multitude of counselors there is safety."

—Proverbs 11:14

"For it was not an enemy that reproached me; then I could have borne it; neither was it he that hated me that did magnify himself against me; then I would have hid myself from him; But it was thou, a man mine equal, my guide, and mine acquaintance. We took sweet counsel together, and walked unto the house of God in company."

—Psalms 55: 12–14

Thoughts

In the next action step, you become an effective coach for the people you lead. This coaching process occurs at three levels: feedback on current performance, feedback to improve performance, and coaching for career enhancement.

Feedback on Performance

It is impossible to overemphasize the importance of giving people feedback on their performance. The research on this is powerful and compelling. Many studies show that it stands out—waaaaay out—beyond anything else in influencing people's productivity. Unfortunately, when you say "performance feedback" to many managers, they assume you mean an annual performance appraisal. And we all know that performance appraisals are unevenly done and sometimes do more harm than good.

Performance feedback simply means ways for employees to know how they're doing. People need information that tells them how their performance compares to other people's and to the expectations of those above them. Some of these mechanisms can be reports that describe the quantity and quality of their output. Salespeople get feedback, such as how many sales they make per month and the size of their orders. To that can be added customer feedback mechanisms. People in manufacturing operations often have excellent feedback because the nature of their work makes measurement easy.

But most people have no feedback tool that lets them know how they're performing. Scott Myers uses the metaphor of driving golf balls into a fogbank. It's not much fun. He also describes rolling bowling balls down a curtained alley, so that you haven't the faintest idea how many pins you knocked over. Without good feedback mechanisms, people's participation in sports would dry up. It's the immediate feedback that is so engaging about most sports activities.

The table on page 101 shows those factors that are barriers to productivity.

The table shows the primary causes of deficient performance. Nearly two-thirds (60 percent) of the companies that responded identified poor or insufficient performance feedback as the main cause. The next biggest causes were high individual stress levels (chosen by only 40 percent of the companies) and no

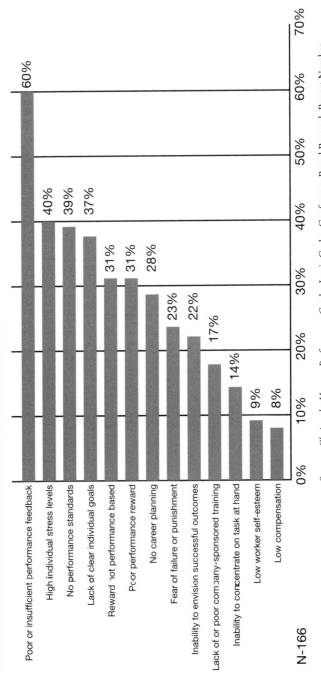

Primary Causes of Deficient Performance
By Percentage of Companies Identifying Various Causes

Poor or insufficient performance feedback — 60%
High individual stress levels — 40%
No performance standards — 39%
Lack of clear individual goals — 37%
Reward not performance based — 31%
Poor performance reward — 31%
No career planning — 28%
Fear of failure or punishment — 23%
Inability to envision successful outcomes — 22%
Lack of or poor company-sponsored training — 17%
Inability to concentrate on task at hand — 14%
Low worker self-esteem — 9%
Low compensation — 8%

N-166

Source: *Closing the Human Performance Gap* by Louis Csoka, Conference Board Research Report Number 1065–94-RR, p. 20, chart 7.

performance standards (chosen by 39 percent). This chart shows that many of our middle- and lower-performing people don't know what they should be doing. Obviously, our current orientation and training processes are not clear enough. What better mechanism could exist than to show them how a star performer functions and say, "Do exactly what you see him or her do."

In addition to feedback in the form of quantities and objective data, people usually want to know how their leader feels about their performance. Is the leader satisfied? Ecstatic? Troubled? This is especially important to new people, who may know the exact quantifiable information about their performance but have no way of interpreting what that means. So the leader has a big opportunity to give meaning to the numbers that the associate receives.

Feedback to Improve Performance

In addition to "How am I doing?" and "How do you feel about it?," most front-line associates want to know "How can I do it better?" Great coaches observe what others do and suggest ways to do it even better in the future. Unfortunately, many people in business keep these ideas to themselves and don't share their wisdom and experience. That's precisely what front-line people complain about and why they feel the lack of performance feedback.

An engineer joined a new firm. During work team meetings he was quiet, but later would go into his manager's office to state his disagreement with decisions that were made. After three episodes of this, the manager decided to coach the new engineer regarding this behavior. The manager took the engineer to lunch and described what she saw happening. The engineer readily agreed and explained that in his former firm open disagreement was punished. People always lobbied for their ideas through back channels or privately with their boss. The manager explained that the culture in the new company was the exact reverse. Everyone expected people to be upfront and say what they thought in the meeting—not later in the hallways. His peers resented his being quiet when they knew he had opinions that weren't being stated.

The manager noticed a dramatic change in the engineer's meeting behavior. While it took two months to make a major turnabout, the change began immediately.

Coaching for Career Enhancement

There's a final kind of coaching that most employees want to receive from time to time. It needn't occur as frequently as coaching on performance issues, but it can't be ignored.

Front-line associates want to know how to get ahead in the organization. How can they be more valuable and earn more opportunities? They want to make themselves more marketable, both inside and outside the company. They look to their immediate leader for this career coaching. They want to know what additional skills they need and what training or education would benefit them.

The contract of lifelong employment no longer exists. Something must replace it, and the replacement contract that people have a right to expect is that the company and their immediate leader will assist them in becoming increasingly effective and marketable. If a downturn occurs and the firm lays them off, their security comes from their capabilities.

"I think you don't change a culture. I think you coach people to win."

Lawrence A. Bossidy, CEO, Allied Signal

Things to Do

1   Get new employees off to the right start by having extensive discussions about performance expectations. These might include questions like:

   • What are the major outputs of your job?

   • How are these measured?

- How could you most easily collect this data?

- What work processes are you responsible for?

- What have you done to streamline that process?

- What unnecessary steps exist in any of the work processes you're involved with?

- What have you done to learn from the top performers around you?

- What parts of your job are you doing more rapidly today than a month ago?

- What's the level of improvement?

- What slows work down in your department?

- What are three significant facts you know about our end-use customer?

- How does that information influence how you function?

Add some general questions like: If you owned the company, what changes would you make in your job?

These are just a few items from over 100 probing questions found in a managers' discussion guide for my book *Not Just for CEOs;* (Irwin Professional Publishing 1996). Such questions provide a vehicle for managers' coaching and performance feedback.

2   Create feedback mechanisms that let people know—in precise terms—how they're doing. Everyone should have one or more measures of how well they're performing. It's best if that information comes directly from the original source rather than from you. Let's face it, most managers have a murky view of the day-to-day performance of their people. It's rare that the leader has timely, objective, and accurate data about the performance of his or her employees. In fact, it's been shown time and again that peers have a much better idea of each other's performance than do bosses.

3　Schedule frequent discussions with each of your subordinates and structure the discussion so that you can give specific, accurate performance feedback. Let them know how you *feel* about their performance.

4　Give your people pointers on how they can be even more effective on the job. Tell them where they can go for help in improving their future performance, such as finding other peak performers from whom they can learn.

5　Provide suggestions on the style or manner in which they do their work. Often people who have the potential to be highly productive have some interpersonal rough spots that get in their way. Coach them on their participation in group meetings or their interactions with people in other departments. People want coaching, not only on what they have accomplished, but also on how they have gone about it.

6　Provide broader career counseling. Help your employees think about career objectives and what they need to do to meet them. What further training do they need? What education would help them?

7　Help them develop job aids that serve as constant reminders of the behavior you want them to exhibit. Checklists, reminders, or summary cards that fit in a pocket or purse can help to lock in the new behavior.

8　Show new people the learning curve that defines the level of performance you expect over time. It will reassure them to know that they aren't expected to perform like an experienced hand immediately. In the process, you can make clear your longer-term high expectations for them.

"Our chief want in life is somebody who will make us do what we can."

Ralph Waldo Emerson

Tips & Afterthoughts

Providing frequent coaching clears the air between you and your employees. It builds a stronger relationship as you focus on helping them develop in the organization. Always think of what information you can give that will either help them perform their tasks more effectively or enhance their career. Much of the stress of a job goes away when people have adequate, accurate information about how they're doing.

Many people worry constantly about what they can't do on the job. Policies and manuals have long lists of don'ts. What really helps people is to see the freedom they have. What *can* they do? Where are the outer boundaries of creativity and innovation that they haven't explored yet?

Such discussions work best if the leader can put them in a framework of *development* instead of evaluation. When the front-line associates realize that your purpose is to help them rather than judge them, the conversation has an entirely different tone. One manager was asked by a senior officer how it was that he never had people on probation and had never had to terminate anyone for poor performance. (Everyone recognized that this manager's team performed extremely well.) The manager's reply? "Oh, I don't do anything all that unusual. If I notice that someone's performance is slipping, I tell them what I've observed. I explain that I don't want to give a negative performance appraisal, and we discuss what that person will need to do to get a positive appraisal."

This manager was an excellent coach, and his discussions with direct reports were always seen as well-intentioned. They were developmental, not evaluative and judgmental.

Coaching is also valuable to your boss. Honest feedback given for the purpose of improving future performance is just as valuable going upward as it is downward or sideways in an organization. Secure leaders welcome this important perspective on what they're doing.

Part 4

Give People the Tools
to Perform

*"The mechanic that would perfect his work
must first sharpen his tools."*

Confucius

Productivity increases when the people in your organization have the necessary skills. Chapter 17 describes the benefits of training, development, and education to both the company and your people. The past decade has seen a growing trend toward teamwork and team-based structures. Chapter 18 describes the benefits of teamwork and the hurdles in getting there.

Chapter 19 encourages leaders to seek the best technology for the area they're in and not count on anyone else (including the information technology department) to stay abreast of technology for them. Chapter 20 is about job aids or performance support systems, a less well-known means of improving productivity. Both manual and electronic support systems are discussed.

Meetings are universally described as time wasters and a drag on productivity. Chapter 21 tells how leaders can run crisper, more substantive, and more productive meetings. The final chapter describes the challenges of putting all the action steps together.

CHAPTER 17 Train, Train, Gain

"Human resources are the primary factor of economic production. Machinery and financial capital are little more than artifacts of the human imagination. Human resource development is the primary lever for improving the nation's overall economic performance and productivity."

—Jackson Grayson, quoting from the 1983 White House Conference on Productivity. Training and Development Journal, January 1984.

Thoughts

What causes a person to be highly productive? It is the combination of skills and knowledge applied in a specific environment. That environment can contain potholes and hurdles to performance, or it can be supportive and nurturing. But without basic skills and knowledge, people can never reach peak productivity.

If you are a savvy businessperson, where are you going to invest money? Where it reaps greatest return. I'm convinced that one of those places is training the work force. All the data I've seen confirms that investments in training and education have a better return on investment than investments in technology, facilities, marketing programs, or even R&D.

> **"The more people learn, the more useful they can be."**
> *David Ogilvy*

Training and Education

Such learning includes both training (which prepares people for today's job or one they're about to enter) and education, which is longer term and designed to give basic skills. Both have been shown to be extremely valuable.

Challenges and Payoffs from Training

Training has huge payoffs, despite the fact that much of what we spent on training in years gone by was wasted. It wasn't job-related. It didn't change behavior. It was delivered at the wrong time, using shoddy methods, and didn't link to the strategic objectives of the firms. It paid off anyway, and now with far better techniques of delivery and more practical content, the payoffs will be greater.

The need for training is enormous. Global competition, a changing work force, new organizational forms, and new technology all place huge demands on our people. If a smaller work force in a downsized organization is going to get all the work done, we need to upgrade their skills.

But the challenge goes way beyond simply teaching new skills. We need to help people unlearn all the wrong things we've taught them in the past. For example, many of our people were punished when they spoke up and made suggestions. They were ignored, told not to rock the boat, and treated like children.

Then a new management team comes along. It wants people to participate, offer suggestions, innovate, take risks, and behave like adults. You've got to find a way to have workers unlearn what they were taught before. You need to extinguish those old feelings and attitudes. Not an easy task, I submit.

We're asking these people to take on expanded roles at the same time we're downsizing. We're asking them to move from a traditional, functional organization structure to focus on work processes. Wow! That's also a lot to ask, especially if we don't give them a way to learn new skills.

Finally, nearly all productivity improvement programs are built around some forms of increasing employee involvement. But many of these people have never acquired the skills of finding problems, collecting data, considering alternatives, and solving problems with a group of peers. They haven't learned the skills of listening, setting priorities, presenting their ideas in a group, and working with people in other departments.

The challenge is staggering.

But let me remind you of the payoffs. Published research tells us that as training boosted workers' wages by 4 to 11 percent, the firms generated profits twice as large as the pay hikes. One study showed that a 10 percent increase in training expenditures produced a 3 percent productivity improvement.

"There are compelling economic reasons to invest in training the work force. Research shows that learning on the job accounted for more than half the productivity increases in the Unites States between 1929 and 1989. In that period, learning was twice as important as technology in boosting productivity and twice as important as formal education."

E. Denison, Brookings Institution, Accounting for United States Economic Growth, 1974, 1976, 1985, 1988.

> **"Additional research shows that people who are trained formally in the workplace have a 30 percent higher productivity rate after one year than people who are not formally trained."**
>
> *J. Bishop, "Achievement, Test Scores, and Relative Wages, "Conference paper, American Enterprise Institute for Public Policy Research, 1969.*

Training is not an end. Knowledge is not an end. Even skill is not the end. What we're after is improved performance right now. Period. If training doesn't do that, then it has failed.

Payoffs from Education

Education is also a terrific investment. One researcher demonstrated that an additional year of high school added $96,000 to a person's career earnings. A Princeton study of identical twins, separated at birth, showed that each additional year of schooling produced a 16 percent increase in wages. The dollar investment made in going to college generated a solid 10 percent per year return. Not bad. Encourage all employees to take classes, participate in company-sponsored training, and continually pursue learning and education. It pays off for them and for you.

In February 1995 the National Center for Educational Quality of the Workforce at the University of Pennsylvania released a study that showed that, on average, a 10 percent increase in an employee's education level resulted in an 8.6 percent gain in productivity. In comparison, a 10 percent increase in the book value of the firm through the increase of capital equipment resulted in only a 3.4 percent increase in productivity. In nonmanufacturing companies this effect was magnified; a 10 percent increase in education (slightly more than one school year) resulted in an 11 percent step-up in productivity.

"We will not get productivity if we do not engage ourselves in the education process both inside and outside our companies."

Jack Welch, chairman, General Electric

As business leaders, we must give the same support to our front-line people's ability and desire to get further education as we do to their training. We must also give emphasis to developing managers. How that's done best is described by one management expert:

"Management schools will begin the serious training of managers when skill training takes a serious place next to cognitive learning.

Cognitive learning no more makes a manager than it does a swimmer. The latter will drown the first time she jumps into the water if her coach never takes her out of the lecture hall, gets her wet, and gives her feedback on her performance.

We are taught a skill through practice plus feedback, whether in a real or a simulated situation. Our management schools need to identify the skills managers use, select students who show potential in these areas, put the students into situations where these skills can be practiced and developed, and then give them systematic feedback on their performance."

Henry Mintzbert "The Manager's Job: Folklore and Fact" HARVARD BUSINESS REVIEW, March–April 1990, no. 2.

Things to Do

1　Make a commitment to invest in training. The best-managed, most progressive companies are the ones investing the most in training. Motorola sets aside 3.6 percent of payroll for training. Corning requires that people spend 5 percent of their work time on training. Andersen Consulting sets aside a whopping 6.8 percent of payroll to train its staff. GE spends 5 percent of direct payroll costs.

2　Decide what strategic initiatives you need to support through a better trained work force. For most companies, this comes down to improved productivity, better quality, improved customer service, or movement to a team structure.

"Training should not be considered without having productivity improvement in mind as a principal goal.

Training thus becomes an integral part of almost any productivity improvement effort. As such training and productivity improvement share a common objective—to improve performance on individual as well as collective levels, thereby increasing efficiency, quality and output while simultaneously controlling (reducing) costs."

Samuel McClelland, Industrial Management, July/August 1993, pp 15–18.

3　Conduct training needs assessment that ferrets out the skills your people require. (I wish we'd change that term to *opportunity assessment.* "Needs" sounds like people are terribly deficient in some basic skill, and that isn't always the issue. The question is, "What skills and knowledge could we give people that would have a high payoff in meeting our strategic initiative?") These assessments can be done by job analysis, surveys, personal observations, interviews, and focus groups.

4   Immediately get people up to the minimum standards required by their job. We've all seen really good people who were dedicated and bright but who lacked education or training. They couldn't read well. They couldn't understand a blueprint. They couldn't perform basic math calculations or understand financial reports. Working with community colleges, I've seen some near miracles occur when these people were exposed to the right kind of education and training. They saw its relevance to their job—right now.

5   Make training mandatory. I know that's controversial. But lots of the Fortune 500 have been doing it for years. When you're made a manager in IBM or GE, it isn't up to you to decide whether you'd enjoy, or whether it's a convenient time for you to go to, a training program to prepare you for your new assignment. It's too easy to find excuses to postpone going to training because of the extreme pressures of work—especially your new job. So wise executives in those companies solved the problem with mandatory training. Participants don't need to feel guilty about getting personal development in order to perform their new job.

6   Purchase the best training available from outside suppliers. Buy from suppliers that sell proven materials or from the local community college or vo-tech school. It's like purchasing computer software. If you can find something that works, meets 80 percent of your needs, and is ready today, then get it. It's cheaper and immediately available.

You'll need to develop some training materials that address unique situations to your organization, but the cost of materials is a trivial part of the total expense of training. The big costs are time off the job, trainers, and facilities.

Maximize the returns from training by using excellent training materials with good internal trainers or contracting to have training delivered by outsiders.

7   Give serious consideration to high-quality computer-based, interactive multimedia training. Self-instructional materials using multimedia technology produce the same results as instructor-led sessions, but often in 30 to 40 percent less time. If you can afford to have multimedia training developed specifically for you, it will save you money in the long run, though the initial investment is higher.

8   Devise a master plan. Don't try to get by with piecemeal training. Develop a two- or three-year strategy for training.

9   Make sure the content is practical. Help people acquire skills, not feelings. In Chapter 14, I recommended finding top performers and having them teach the other people in their work group exactly what they do. That's the kind of practicality I'm talking about. Training should do what it purports to do. If it doesn't, then dump it.

10   Reinforce what people learn with other systems in the organization. Have performance appraisal systems evaluate the same skills covered in training. Design the compensation system to reward people who practice what they learn in training. Help people see near-term, obvious payoffs from practicing what they're being taught.

11   Make certain the training is delivered in a highly interactive, engaging fashion. Sitting and listening to a lecture isn't the best way to learn. Harvard Medical School tested its fourth-year students on what they'd learned in their first-year science classes. They remembered 15 percent of it.

Create situations where people can make mistakes and learn from their experience. Load the training with lots of cases, stories, examples, and parables. People remember those.

12   Don't jam training into one large clump. When you space learning out over time it gets digested better and sticks with you. Six half-days spaced apart is superior to three days in a row.

13   Train people to behave under adverse circumstances, not just in a safe, sanitary classroom situation. The real test of a skill is whether workers can use it when they're pressed for time or an angry customer is yelling at them.

14   Combine technical training with soft-skill training. Both are needed, for many people and the soft skills are the hard ones to learn.

15   Measure the results of your training efforts. Motorola has publicly stated that over three years, it recoups $30 for every dollar invested in training. Get some idea of what your payoff is. It will help protect that investment when an accountant raises the question.

"Companies that increased their training budgets after work-force reductions were twice as likely to show increased profits and productivity than companies that cut their training expenses."

American Management Assn. Survey, June 30, 1995

---

16   Encourage everyone to pursue lifelong learning and formal education. It is essential for success in today's world.

Tips & Afterthoughts

The overall training effort ought to help people stretch personally, improve results for their part of the business, and improve their leadership skills.

Be an active participant in the training process. Kick off the first session with every new group. Pass out the graduation certificates. Drop by and lend your support to what is being taught. Discuss with your subordinates how they're applying what they've learned. That's what support from leaders is all about.

We sometimes think that training is only for those who are skill deficient. But here's a different view:

"The better you are, the more training and learning you need."

Peter Drucker

One of the most gratifying results of any company's training efforts are the reports from employees who are able to use their new skills at home. When you teach people how to listen and communicate better at work, they'll take those skills home.

One man told me after a training course that he was now talking to his teenage daughter, who hadn't spoken to him in six months. Marriages improve. Families are strengthened because we've made our people more skillful.

In today's world of downsizing and restructuring, there is a question about the nature of the new implied contract between organizations and their people. It certainly isn't lifetime employment anymore. Training plays an important role in the new contract, because it signals to our people that we care about them, we want to see them progress, we want them to be marketable, and we're willing to invest in them.

Separate training problems from motivational problems. Bob Mager proposed the acid test: If you put a gun to a person's head and said you were going to shoot unless they performed a certain task, could they? If they *could* do it, then it wasn't a training problem. It was a motivational problem. We're forever trying to solve motivational problems with training, and it just doesn't work very well.

Team-based structures call for an entirely new set of skills for team members and team leaders. Many organizations that implemented self-directed work teams discovered that training consumed roughly one-fourth of their time in the first year and then leveled out to about 5 percent of their time. Without extensive training, the team initiatives will fail.

View training as a process, not an event. Training isn't a class. It's a long-term commitment to improve performance.

As Maxwell Maltz said, "We're all like bicycle riders. If we're not going forward, we tip over." We have to help our people keep moving forward. Training is a great way to do that.

CHAPTER 18 Grow Teams

"Why Teams? Because it makes the most money for the business. You do it with less employees, a higher quality product, less staff, quicker turnaround time, faster delivery and speedier decisions.

The rude awakening of American management is going to come when employers demand this instead of simply suggesting it."

—*Mike Southard, vice president, Wesley-Jessen*

Thoughts

The next action item involves teams. Why? Because they work. As a rule, productivity goes up 30 to 50 percent over a period of time if they're implemented well.

"I guarantee that when someone says teams don't work, it's because management did not take an interest."

James Watson, vice president, Texas Instruments

Don't confuse teamwork with teams. People who work together develop a collaborative spirit. That's a terrific first step. Teamwork is an essential foundation. It's the essence of cooperation and the opposite of competition. But displaying signs of teamwork is not enough to make a team.

Our society reveres competition. We attribute our economic success to it. We extend it from the sports world to school, and from school to work. But people who believe competition drives a company's productivity are dead wrong (especially if they're talking about competition inside the organization).

Many firms encourage fierce fighting and competition inside and maintain relatively cordial relations with competitors. Sports teams are just the opposite. Winners have incredible cooperation within the team; they save competition for the teams they play against.

While a short-term contest between departments can successfully spur performance, it can't be allowed to continue for long. Superior performance inside a company comes from extensive cooperation and the complete dismissal of internal competition. That fact has been proved over and over with businesspeople, college students, elementary school students, airplane pilots, reservation clerks. In all these studies cooperation always wins.

Why? Because in collaboration people share resources and information. In competition, they hide information from each other, squirrel away resources, and even stoop to giving out misinformation and stealing resources. Collaboration brings out a broader range of skills.

Finally, if you're competing with someone you are thinking about how to beat them—how to win at all costs. That's totally different from thinking about being productive—producing the highest-quality product in the most efficient way and achieving the greatest output with the least input.

We do better on tasks we enjoy and that we're doing for sound reasons. When winning gets in the way, the pure enjoyment of the task gets lost in the fight. The real activity takes a backseat to the contest.

To make teams succeed, the first principle that the organization must agree to is emphasizing cooperation and collaboration and minimizing competition. The second agreement you need to get is that the basic building block of your company is not Bill, Mary, and Joe. It's teams of people working together. That's the foundation on which any healthy organization stands. There are precious few solo jobs left in companies today. The third agreement needs to be on the fundamental principle that you'll encourage cooperation, not just within teams, but between teams inside your organization.

Why Teams Are Now Possible

Two academicians, Zenger and Hesterly, argued that team-based structures have been made possible because of new technology that allows better measurement and monitoring, including customer satisfaction audits, product quality measures, benchmarking, measures of timeliness, and activity-based accounting.

"These new performance measures can be the basis for compensation and rewards. Consequently, considerably less hierarchical governance is required."[5]

Teams and Productivity

I noted earlier that teams increase productivity. That's because teams make better decisions over the long haul and in more circumstances than any one person—including their best and brightest member. Teams create high levels of involvement and participation, which we've always known paid off but didn't know how to achieve.

Teams create havens for people. Most people like to belong to a group. Healthy personalities want friends and colleagues. Teams provide necessary human interaction through a workday. Solitary confinement is a terrible punishment.

---

[5] Todd Zenger and William Hesterly, "The Disaggregation of Corporations: Selective Intervention, High-Powered Incentives, and Molecular Units," *Organization Science,* forthcoming 1996.

But the biggest advantage of teams is that they encourage front-line people to accept responsibility. Employees feel like owners. Once you get teams started, turning back can be difficult.

If you teach a bear to dance with you, you must be prepared to keep dancing until the bear chooses to stop.

If you implement a team-based organization, it will be extremely difficult to go back to the old structure.

Things to Do

1 Determine if your culture is ready for teams. The steps we talked about earlier are exactly the right preparation for teams. The culture has to include open communication, relatively high levels of trust between front-line people and management, and minimal layers.

2 Define where teams can function. Not every activity is compatible with teams. Try the classic 3-t test. Are the people together in *time?* (It's hard to have teams of people working widely different hours.) Are they in the same *territory?* (Teams work best when people physically see each other and connect frequently during the day.) Do they share *technology?* (Are they using the same equipment and performing the same tasks, or tasks that connect with each other?)

3 Determine how ready and willing the people in the organization are to work in a team structure. Managers need to stop telling people what to do and giving them the answers to problems. They must change to asking questions and helping others to do the problem solving. That's a big leap for some of us. Teams mean big changes for the front-line people too. They need to have more skills and accept more responsibility.

Dental students are usually challenged by operating in a small space while looking into a mirror. Their natural instinct is to move in the opposite direction. Working in teams calls for some behavior that is the opposite of past behavior that we learned while working in a competitive (everyone for himself) culture.

4   Have honest talks with all of the people you're thinking of involving to find out if they're really with you.

5   Clean up work processes. A well-motivated team performing a dysfunctional work process is not going to succeed in the long run. They'll be doing the wrong thing really well. Fix the process first.

6   Set clear expectations for results. Teams aren't just a pleasant social experiment being done to amuse management. They need to be implemented for a sound business reason. Teams can do the job better. But "the job" has to be described in great detail, with clear expectations for quantity, quality, timeliness, costs, customer satisfaction (or whatever the right measures are for that group).

7   Train team members to perform new tasks. Experience shows that two things can kill a team quickly. One is your lack of support. The other is lack of ample training for the people on the teams.

That training must include technical skills, but it goes way beyond that. Team members need new interpersonal skills to help them work together effectively. They also need administrative skills, such as requesting maintenance to fix a machine, getting supplies, or requisitioning temporary help. Don't just announce teams, name the people, and then abandon them without the skills they'll need to succeed.

8   Allow ample time. Getting teams up and running doesn't happen in a day, a week, or even a month. Don't be impatient.

> **"We now know where productivity, real and limitless, comes from. It comes from challenged, empowered, excited, rewarded teams of people."**
>
> *Jack Welch, chairman of GE*

Tips & Afterthoughts

Teams generate a wide array of new behavior from front-line people. Response time improves, quality goes up, greater flexibility occurs, cycle times are reduced, and people become more innovative. These elements add up to higher productivity.

For decades, we've talked about participation and involvement of our front-line people. Teams are a structural way to make involvement happen.

The biggest mistake reported by companies moving to teams is the immediate departure of former supervisors or managers. Moving to teams should constitute a gradual process. Managers should pass on to teams just what they're ready to handle. The managers involvement should always be developmental; they mustn't meddle and second guess. This is where they'll need consummate coaching skills.

This topic is so important—and sufficiently complex—that you may want to read some more material on the subject. I suggest four books.

Self-Directed Work Teams: The New American Challenge. Jack D. Orsburn, Linda Moran, Ed Musselwhite, and John H. Zenger. Homewood, IL: Business One Irwin, 1990.

The Wisdom of Teams. Jon R. Katzenbach and Douglas K. Smith. Boston, MA: Harvard Business School Press, 1993.

Leading Teams: Mastering the New Role. John H. Zenger, Ed Musselwhite, Kathleen Hurson, and Craig Perrin. Homewood, IL: Business One Irwin, 1994.

Keeping Teams on Track: What to Do When the Going Gets Rough. Linda Moran, Ed Musselwhite, and John H. Zenger. Burr Ridge, IL: Irwin Professional Publishing, 1996.

CHAPTER 19 Live on the Cutting Edge

"While the potential of technology seems infinite, the road to infinity is rocky."
—*Price Waterhouse LLP, The Paradox Principles*

Thoughts

An important action step is to adapt the best technology. No, you don't want to be the test site for every new idea or tool, because someone will always be pushing cockamamie ideas at you.

But history shows that those who resist new technology lose out. Major new technologies take time to hit their full stride (though that time gets increasingly shorter). When electricity was first introduced to commercial applications, it took 40 years for it to be fully integrated and for the transformation from steam and water power to be complete. Using electricity required new layouts of plants and major reorganizations of how work was done. But when the integration was finished, there was a huge payoff.

It took 50 years for telephones to become a commercial success. We're in the midst of a similar evolution. We're still using old information systems, and we're running new information systems parallel to or on top of the old ones. We're adding to our costs, and that will continue until the transformation is completed and paper-based accounting and information systems are replaced by electronic ones.

The companies that pioneered the new computer technology paid a high price. I'm not only talking about those who invested millions in mainframe computers. I'm also referring to the fact that PCs have proven to be extremely expensive; they can cost up to $40,000 per year if companies add up all the costs of hardware, software, help desks, and support.

The secret is that a new technology must be strong enough to compel a complete reorganization of the firm around it. So far, the information technology groups have usually not had that much clout, and only a few organizations have had the foresight to go all the way. The ones that have are reaping big benefits. Wal-Mart, Mrs. Fields Cookies, Progressive Life Insurance, Charles Schwab, FedEx, Blockbuster—all these companies exploited technology and organized themselves around it. They saw how it could help them serve customers better.

Unfortunately, many executives today see technology as a camel trying to get its nose under the tent. The executives don't understand the camel or what it can do for them, so they let the camel put its head in, but no more. That gives them the worst of both worlds. The tent is drafty, and the camel isn't carrying its load.

You need to seek out and adopt the best technologies and then carefully manage their introduction into the organization. They can't be let loose like an unruly child at a formal dinner. Horror stories abound, but it's even more dangerous to sit by and wait for your competitors to get it all worked out.

Things to Do

1   Make every manager responsible for identifying technology that advances his or her area. The production manager should examine the latest CAD-CAM technologies and the cutting edge of manufacturing technology. Marketing should keep up with the latest technology for analyzing and

segmenting markets. The VP of sales should be conversant with sales force automation tools that make a field force significantly more productive. Human resources should investigate the latest software to manage information about employees, with one central database. (One company discovered that with hiring information, payroll, 401(k) plans, pensions, medical and life insurance benefits, medical exams, bonus plans, training and development programs, performance appraisals and more, its HR department had 30 separate databases, none of which talked to the others.)

2   Encourage managers to get expert help in evaluating the best hardware, software, and other available technology as you approach buying decisions. That's seldom a capability you'll have in-house, but these decisions are so important and far-reaching that it's worth getting expert opinions. You'll avoid costly mistakes.

3   Appoint a chief information officer who is charged with keeping internal information systems up to date. While each manager of a process or functional area should keep his or her own area at the cutting edge, someone has to pull all of that together. Make certain that internal information technology is available to run the firm. For example, the new groupware software packages can provide an enormous leg up in keeping committees functioning effectively, because work can occur even when people are in different time zones. These technologies change how people interact. A study of 65 firms using Lotus Notes showed an average return on investment of 179 percent. Similar positive results come from sales force automation tools such as Learning International's Heatseeker product.

The interfaces between marketing and sales, manufacturing and sales, and engineering and manufacturing all require constant reinvention.

4   Encourage everyone in the organization to keep abreast of the latest technology that could help them in their job. Workers who use computers earn, on average, 10 to 15 percent more than those who don't. Secretaries adept at using computers earn up to 30 percent more than those who type or merely use simple word processors.

Much of what happens in offices echoes what used to happen in factories. Earlier I noted that in the typical plant, any part or product was being worked on only 5 percent of the time that it took to get through the production cycle. I'll wager that paperwork is about the same.

Moving papers from one person's out-basket to someone else's in-basket, and then to their out-basket, and then into someone else's in-basket is a colossal waste. Your people see that nonsense much better than you can. Get them to point it out and stop it. Give them power to kill needless reports. Eliminate unnecessary approvals. Emancipate people from slavery to outdated systems.

5   Include ample training in any new technology budgets. That's the wrong place to skimp. Computer word-processing and spreadsheet training taught us all a tough lesson. If workers learned on their own, it was estimated to cost $3,000 to $5,000 per person, but if they received some formal training (often self-instructional tapes) the cost was around $1,350. Executives have wasted a lot of time trying to figure out how to print memos or send faxes. Worse yet, many of your people aren't using the full capability of their hardware and software simply because they lack training.

6   Maintain personal connections inside the company. While new technology allows some transitions to happen with less personal contact, don't assume that infinitely less contact is better. As the use of technology goes up, so does the need for periodic human connection. The airlines will prosper along with the telecommunications companies.

Tips & Afterthoughts

Find exciting and powerful new technologies that better link you to your customers. Organize your entire company (or at least many of your functions and work processes) around those technologies even if it means turning yourself inside out. That's where the real payoff will come. If you examine the firms that have made great strides, you'll see that pattern repeated every time.

Information is power. When you give information to all of the people in the front lines of the organization, you empower them. Really secure managers think that's terrific. The fuddy-duddies and bullies lie awake at 3:30 A.M. worrying about their loss of power and control and fearing for their future.

When you introduce new technology, be prepared for how it can change your culture. Many were dismayed by the changes e-mail wrought, for example. Brash anonymous messages were sent to the CEOs. Messages in general were far less respectful of authority. The buttoned-down gentility of the traditional firm suddenly collided with an Internet mentality.

Make certain that using new technology doesn't become the end goal. The point is to use the technology to do a better job and get more real work done. Some people get caught up with gee-whiz toys and forget that using a computer isn't what they're paid for. Critics have pointed out the irony of high-priced executives typing their own memos and sending their own faxes while their secretaries attend meetings. Computers can help designers be much more efficient—if the designers don't spend inordinate amounts of time learning how to use and support the computer rather than doing the design work they were hired to do.

CHAPTER 20 **Keep an Expert Alongside**

"Job aids enrich the work environment, boosting performance by providing employees with information resources.

Job aids are assets that pay immediate dividend when an employer performs a particular task."

—Angie Tilaro and Allison Rossett, "Creating Motivating Job Aids," Performance and Instruction, October 1993, p. 13.

Thoughts

We noted earlier that performance is a combination of a person's skills, abilities, and motivation applied in a work environment. While training improves personal skills and competencies, we also need to strengthen the work environment. One of the best ways to do that is through *job aids,* or performance support tools.

Job Aids

Job aids are devices to enhance performance. They provide instant help to perform a job while you're in the midst of doing it. They are tutors or performance coaches. They provide needed information to workers just in time, just for them, and just their speed. Job aids aren't events that happen in a classroom; they are tools embedded in the work environment, available continually, and giving the learner some combination of text, graphic information, audio, or full-motion video to enhance the learning and immediate performance.

A job aid provides information about a procedure, suggests steps to follow, gives useful information about performing each step, and warns of things to look out for.

The extensive use of job aids take us back to the days of on-the-job training when a personal tutor stood at your work station, coaching you through the new job. But the job aid never loses its patience, never resents being asked the same questions again, and unfailingly gives the right answers.

You Use Them Now

Job aids are not new to you, but the name may be. Here are some basic, maybe even primitive, examples. If you use a time management planner, that's a job aid for organizing work, scheduling activities, tracking accomplishments, and organizing addresses and telephone numbers. If you cook with a recipe, you're familiar with a job aid. The recipe helps you make sure that no ingredient is left out and that everything is in the correct quantity and added in the right sequence. If you make a "to do" list, that's a job aid. Written instructions showing how to assemble a wagon are a job aid.

They Come in Different Formats

The most primitive job aid is a brief manual printed on paper. They range from the size of a business card up to a pamphlet in a worker's pocket to a large poster. They may provide information, outline procedures, prompt the performer at various steps, and coach the reader through difficult procedures. They work as long as they're short, well organized, and customer focused. They're best when they contain pictures, make information easy to find, have clear diagrams, are extremely handy to use, are durable, and contain a bit of humor.

Consider the typical car owner's manual. Most show a tour of the car from the engineers' viewpoint. But what the customer most often needs is help in handling an episode, an event where something has gone wrong. The battery needs replacing. A tire is flat. The car overheats. Maybe that's how the manual should be organized, not from engineering diagrams of the car.

As the world has moved to electronic devices, many job aids have become *electronic performance support systems*. They normally consist of some software, hypertext, expert system elements, and computer-based training. They can be on CD-ROM for one user or on a server so that many people have simultaneous access to the information.

The possibilities seem nearly limitless. From instructions on how to run a machine or how to fix the machine, factory workers are enjoying practical help to learn and do their jobs. Other systems answer the customer service rep's questions about products. Or they prompt the customer service person to ask probing questions of the caller or provide answers to 80 percent of all inquiries from customers.

Finally, some performance tools are being incorporated into the actual products and equipment that workers use. For example, service-station restrooms are cleaned by attendants who usually have little training, especially in cleaning and sanitation. (If they're hired for any skill, it is that they enjoy working on cars.) The chemicals and cleaning solutions are now being combined with job aids that tell the attendant exactly what steps to follow in cleaning the restroom, explaining how and why to perform each step. Kits and carts seamlessly bind together the equipment and the performance support system so that a relatively untrained person can do this job satisfactorily the first time.

Often there is a natural evolution of paper-based tools into electronic ones. Jeppesen-Sanderson is a company headquartered in Englewood, Colorado, and Frankfurt, Germany. It provides flight maps and information to pilots worldwide including detailed instructions regarding take-off and landing in all of the major airports of the world. These instructions began as the handwritten notes of one pilot, Captain "Jepp", who penciled information in a black looseleaf book as he landed at and took off from airports. Soon other pilots asked for these notes. These have now become the standards in the world of aviation, and they are the classic job aid for pilots. Now they are available in computerized form for pilots to view on a screen.

"Accessible information in the world doubles every two to three years."

Allen Kay, author, information technology pioneer

Where Are Such Job Aids Needed?

1   The new worker benefits greatly from having a handy summary of the job steps, needed information, and tutorial help.

2   Anyone about to perform a new task can benefit from performance tools—for example, the new person in accounting who will be closing the books at month-end for the first time. Or the bank representative who is explaining a new financial service to a client for the first time.

> *I went into a bank last week with some Japanese yen I'd brought back from a trip. It took a teller about half an hour to look up in a book the picture of my currency, make the calculations to convert to dollars, get approvals from bank officers, and then give me dollars in return. She had some job aids, but they were cumbersome and time-consuming. Dealing with her was very different from changing currency in a bank at a major airport, where such transactions occur constantly. But at least she was able to do it with the help of job aids.*

3   When we perform an infrequent task, job aids become useful to all of us, regardless of what we do. Conducting a hiring interview or a performance appraisal is such an event

for most managers. Both are extremely important, but few managers do them often enough to get really comfortable. That's the perfect place for a job aid.

The advent of complex telephone and voice mail systems creates challenges for people who don't use those functions often. How do you transfer a call from outside to someone else? Do you press transfer, dial their number, and hang up? Or do you press "transfer" again? How do you put someone on hold and connect up a third party that you'd like to patch into a conversation? The suppliers have created small cards that answer the most common questions. Those are job aids.

I recently bought a compact 35-mm camera. I also have a bulky SLR camera and a video camera. But I don't use any one of them often enough to remember the meaning of all the symbols on the dial or how to execute an infrequent event like rewinding a roll of film midway. Why don't manufacturers supply a small laminated card that I can carry in the camera case, with all of the key information summarized? Sure, I want the manual too but I don't carry manuals with me on a hiking trip or in the park. I need the information to be with me, not on a closet shelf. I'm asking for a practical job aid when I'm outside taking pictures.

4   Many organizations have distributed populations (people scattered thinly all over the country). They're great prospects for job aids or performance support tools.

5   Performance support systems play into the growing autonomy and independence of the work force in general. As workers become more mature, they don't want to constantly ask for directions. They see themselves as adults, not children needing to be instructed at every turn.

6   There are enormous differences in the knowledge and experience of workers. Some need a great deal of help. Others need virtually none. Job aids do away with the need

to giving everyone large doses of training. Traditional training often treats front-line people as one homogenous group, assuming each needs about the same level of information. But that isn't true; huge differences exist. The practice of teaching extensive information about complex jobs through classroom training is increasingly challenged by some leading performance specialists.

Payoffs of Job Aids

Ideally, a performance support system integrates information, tools, methods, and decision aids into "right here, right now" instructions that allow a person to perform to a reasonably high standard quickly—possibly without any other formal training.

The use of such job aids greatly improves people's performance. It saves them the agony of trying to remember exactly how to do something.

"While good job aids look deceptively simple, there is more to them than meets the eye."

S. Zagorski, "The Job Aid as ZEN ART."

Things to Do

1   Enthusiastically endorse the creation and use of job aids and performance support systems for everyone.

2   Seek out high performers and collect the job aids and performance support tools they use.

3   Ask front-line associates information they would like to have instantly available on the job. This may be product information, customer information, technical data, competitor data, market information, financial information, or illustrations of how to handle difficult situations they face on their jobs.

4   Assign teams to create the job aids people need. They usually turn out best when many people have had a hand in creating them.

5   Test the newly created job aids with both new employees and old hands. You'll always get some good refinements.

6   Insist that all workers document their current work procedures. Some people are reluctant to make up job aids and document exactly what they do. They seem to feel greater job security if nothing is written down, especially if they are the sole occupant of the position.

7   Invest in electronic support systems where the number of people and the complexity of the job warrant it.

8   Train people to use job aids. Get them to practice and rehearse using them to ensure their success.

Tips & Afterthoughts

The consequences of not performing well and rewards for excelling should provide additional incentive for employees to use job aids or performance support tools. People who are reluctant must be shown the link between their use of job aids and their performance, and ultimately their compensation and security in their position.

Job aids need to be extraordinarily simple to use. Everyone calculates the payoff from taking certain actions. For example, I often debate whether to look up a question about a computer software program in a manual (or even in the on-screen help tutorials). There's always the trade-off between the time it takes and the knowledge I'll gain. Frankly, looking up often loses. It has to be quick and simple and provide me with really useful information, or I won't do it.

Sometimes we have to be tenacious to get people to document their work or write clear descriptions of what they do on complex assignments. Discussing their reluctance and allaying their concerns about job security help get past that.

Explain that your main reason for wanting documentation and job aids is to help them. You must have this information if they ever want to move on to another job (but obviously you shouldn't imply that this will lead to their promotion).

Their documentation also protects the company and provides a backup when they are ill. Stress that you are not getting ready to outsource their job.

In the process of creating a job aid, people often streamline and simplify their work. There's something about writing it down that leads to improvement.

CHAPTER 21 Make Meetings Meatier

"Meetings have always been an organizational fact of life. What's changing is the role meetings play as employees take responsibility for managing and improving their own work. There's more pressure for meetings to produce results."

—From "Facilitating for Results" by Zenger Miller

Thoughts

Ask any group of businesspeople, "What eats up valuable time and detracts from your productivity?" The first thing out of their mouths is "Meetings, meetings, meetings." Nearly everyone complains about them. Ninety percent of our complaints are about the ones we attend, not the ones we conduct. It may not occur to us that people who report to us are probably just as disparaging of the meetings that we run and they have to attend.

Think back over the last week. How many hours did you personally spend in meetings? It is not unusual for managers and executives to spend half their time in meetings. That's nearly 1,000 hours per year. There are huge opportunities for productivity improvement if these meetings can be made even 10 percent more effective.

What's Wrong with Meetings?

We can all think of meetings where people straggle in. There is no agenda. As latecomers arrive the leader takes time to bring them up to date. This wastes the time of all who were punctual. No times are allotted to items. There is no clarity of purpose for each agenda item. The person leading the meeting is satisfied with simply having discussed a topic. There are no decisions, no closure, and no action plans agreed upon.

People leave extremely frustrated. They perceive that the meeting was a waste of time, expensive overhead frittered away on an unfruitful task.

Unfortunately, the aggregated salaries of the people involved are not the only cost. The largest cost is probably the opportunity of what was missed—what could have been accomplished if the meeting had been run well.

The Role of Meeting Leaders

The leader of a meeting can be a catalyst. Just as the reagent added to a vat of chemicals triggers a major reaction, so effective leaders make an enormous difference in the productivity of the group. When leaders are well prepared and conduct crisp meetings, they convey to participants that they accept responsibility for the outcomes of the meetings. They care about the time of everyone involved. They want to produce the best possible outcomes with a minimum investment.

Things to Do

1   Prepare an agenda. Some organizations have a rule that if there is no agenda there is no meeting. Assemble the agenda by getting inputs from everyone who will attend. Prepare it in advance if possible. At least put it on a board so that everyone can see what items will be discussed, what the objective is for each item, and how much time is allocated to each.

It's like making plans to hike across mountains. You can save enormous amounts of time during the hike if your course is clear, well laid out, and agreed upon in advance.

2   Make sure people understand the objective and desired outcome for each topic on the agenda. Some topics may be there simply to provide information. Others may seek the opinions of everyone for a later decision by someone else. Some items may be there for an exchange of ideas. Still others may require brainstorming or some more complicated problem-solving technique. Explain the desired outcome for each topic and give an estimate of the time it will take. Encourage people to ask about objectives if they are not entirely clear.

3   Manage the process. The leader's job is to make sure the meeting goes well. Don't give all the opinions, provide all the information, or make all the decisions. There is no law of physics that says good ideas float upward in an organization.

Make sure that the meeting stays on track, that people are participating, that sufficient information is available, that background documents are on the table in advance, that the meeting maintains a reasonable pace, and that good spirits prevail.

Good leaders listen and observe and then fill in the missing pieces of the process. They ask questions if the group is moving forward without good information. They serve as gatekeepers, making sure each person's contribution is equal to their participation. They bring the quiet people into the conversation. To the person who hogs too much air time, they say gently, "I'd like to hear what Mary has to say on this topic."

The leader should not take minutes of the meeting. That should be delegated or a volunteer requested to take "action minutes," which summarize items that are decided and need follow-up in future meetings.

If you truly seek the ideas and opinions of other people, try to withhold your comments until others have had a chance to speak. Ask questions and let other members of the group carry the content while you manage the process.

4   Keep the meeting moving at a brisk pace. Otherwise people become inattentive and their thoughts wander off. You can increase the pace by periodically summarizing where the group is and asking if others agree. Or ask others to summarize. Inviting a person to give further information enriches the group's understanding. Encourage those who are not participating to speak up. Presumably people were invited to attend because they had something to contribute. If they don't participate, then their reason for attending has been lost.

5   Encourage diverse views. If everyone in the meeting states the same view, what was the point of having a meeting? Encourage people with different points of view to speak up. Protect the viewpoints of those who are shy and vulnerable, especially ideas that are contrary to popular opinion.

    Do not let people derail the meeting. Your job is to deal with disruptive behavior. That can often be done by agreeing on ground rules in advance and then asking the group to evaluate how their behavior is conforming to them.

6   Nail down decisions and action plans. As the meeting progresses and decisions are made, assign tasks to those who are responsible. People will leave with a feeling of accomplishment if specific actions are assigned and results follow.

7   Plan to follow up at agreed-upon times to see if you are making progress. The minutes should reflect all decisions that have been made. The leader accepts responsibility for organizing the follow-up steps that ensure each of the items will be accomplished.

8   Periodically hold a postmortem in your meetings. Invite people to speak up and reflect on the overall success of the meeting from their point of view. At the end of every meeting, take a few minutes to ask people for their honest reactions to the meeting.

Tips & Afterthoughts

It takes a really good meeting to be better than no meeting at all. If the proper preparations are not made and the right people can't attend, it is often better not to schedule any meeting.

Make everyone share responsibility for the success of meetings. When things are not going well, everyone should be encouraged to speak up and propose ways to get the meeting back on track. The meeting belongs to everyone, and others may be in the best position to improve its quality.

If you aren't hearing diverse points of view, you are really missing the point. You are the protector of the timid people. In many meetings there are a few rhinoceroses who stomp the ground, snort loudly, and charge at everything that moves. There are usually some turtles too. When attacked, they pull in their head and all four legs and wait for the threat to pass. But with head and legs pulled in, turtles aren't really big contributors. They need to be protected from rhinoceroses, especially in the early stages of the meeting, until they become more comfortable with each other.

The leader is the catalyst that can make remarkable things happen. If the meeting is not going well, the leader must accept responsibility. It would be nice if every meeting created the magic of $1+1+1+1=10$. Unfortunately, the reality is that many meetings consist of $1+1+1+1=2$.

CHAPTER 22 Spin All the Plates

"You'll never plough a field by turning it over in your mind."

—*Irish Proverb*

What's the key to achieving peak productivity? It's taking all of the 21 action steps described in this book. They need to be executed well and integrated together.

Simultaneous Actions Are Required

Achieving our desired result becomes a matter of going back and doing these things over and over again. It's like painting the Golden Gate Bridge. They start painting at one end and by the time they get to the other end, they have to start all over again. It's a neverending process. That's exactly what's required to bring about successful organizational transformation.

I know these 22 recommendations seem like a lot. Wouldn't it be nice if you could do just one thing and have everything get better? One silver bullet! One dose of magic elixir—and the company would be better forever. But we all know that's not how the world works.

Instead, you are much more like the circus performer who is spinning plates. Just as the performer gets to the eighth plate spinning on a rod, the first one begins to wobble. The performer races back and revives that one and the ones next to it—then races down to the end to get one more plate up and spinning. While that's largely showmanship, the reality of organization transformation is that you must get many worthwhile things going simultaneously. While you're working on the new plates, the first ones will get wobbly and need reviving. So you'll be running back to some of the things you started first. The good news is that the whole becomes greater than the sum of its parts. Keep those plates going as best you can and you'll see miraculous things occur.

Productivity Is a Leadership Issue

What can leaders affect? These elements can be categorized into three large clusters.

- People.
- How work is organized and gets done.
- Organization culture.

I would submit that until now we've done it exactly backwards. Managers have placed most of their emphasis on controlling the people, but they paid little attention to streamlining work and processes, and done little to improve the culture.

But workers can't unilaterally change work processes, the structure of their jobs, or the organization culture. That's where they need their manager's help. When managers create a good, nurturing environment for the front-line people, their internal motivation can blossom.

The 10,000 workers that Jay Hall of Teleometrics studied consistently said they wanted an environment that facilitated high productivity. Those workers knew what they needed to create that environment: collaboration, trust, access to information, more personal contact, the elimination of formal and bureaucratic policies, an end to irrelevant activities, a chance to demonstrate their competence and use their minds.

But the actual conditions supplied by management were exactly the opposite—*competence suppressors*. These policies, practices, and procedures punished and prevented any expressions of competence. The workers placed their own organizations at the 17th percentile in providing the needed support for highly productive efforts.

So all the time when management should have been finding ways to make work more efficient and to improve the overall organization culture, it was wasting energy controlling people. The best executives have learned their lesson. They're getting out of their workers' way. They're focusing on the things that only they can manage and giving more responsibility and involvement to the people inside. The results are spectacular!

Employee Satisfaction and Productivity

For years we've debated the relationship between employee satisfaction and productivity. As best I can tell, there is no evidence that when employee satisfaction goes up beyond a threshold level, productivity inevitably follows. We've all seen "country clubs" where employees are blissfully content but minimally productive.

However, there is evidence that when productivity escalates, employee satisfaction goes up. That's intuitive to most people. Everyone enjoys being on a winning team. Productive organizations can afford to treat their people better. The steps that lead to productivity also build a better work culture. Whatever the reasons, if you succeed in pushing up productivity, you can bank on having more satisfied workers. And they'll provide better customer service as a consequence.

National Consequences

The impact of such growth on our economy could be profound. The most obvious impact would be on our standard of living. If productivity increases in the past two decades had matched those prior to 1970, we'd all be enjoying a 25 percent better living

standard. Better houses, cars, education, vacations, medical care—
everything would be one-quarter better. Our overwhelming
national debt would be eradicated. Interest rates would plummet,
making it easier for people to buy homes and cars.

Company Consequences

Look at the companies like GE or Cisco Systems which have
achieved high productivity growth rates and you get a glimpse of
what that achievement means. It makes them more profitable and
much more competitive. Their profitability allows them to hire and
keep the best people. They can afford to pay the best wages. They
can invest more in R&D. They can purchase necessary capital
equipment and the latest in technology. Literally everything goes
better for the company.

Personal Consequences

But most important, how do we help today's work force? For the
overwhelmingly greatest number of people, their pay has actually
diminished in real wages after adjustments for inflation. Overall,
wages have kept pace with inflation. But that's only because the
top 20 percent of earners are doing extremely well. Meanwhile, a
growing percentage of people at the bottom of the earning curve
are living below the poverty level. Those in the middle work
longer, harder, and often with two wage earners in a household
in order to stay afloat as their real wages decline.

Increasing productivity is a major key to assuring workers
incomes that keep up with the cost of living. Increasing
productivity is also the best hope for people to spend fewer
hours to produce more.

A 1996 *Wall Street Journal*/NBC News survey showed 32
percent of American workers were working 50 hours per week or
more. In contrast to previous generations where people with
money were the leisure class, today finds people who earn more

than $100,000 per year saying that managing time is a bigger problem than managing money. The only people with lots of leisure time are those on the lowest rung of the economic ladder.

Our society is paying a high price in the disintegration of family structure and declining personal quality of life. If there is an answer to that riddle. it would seem to lie in our ability to produce more quality goods and services in less time and with less hassle. It is clear that some people have learned how to do that. It is time for all leaders to take this issue seriously and initiate productivity improvement activities.

Index

154   Index

Dear Reader:

If you found this book valuable as a leader in your company, you should know about a companion book by the same author. *Not Just for CEOs* was written for the front-line person in your organization—clerks, customer service representatives, salespeople, factory workers, accountants—anyone who doesn't have supervisory or managerial responsibility. The message is the "other side of the coin" from what you've just read. It describes what that group needs to do to boost productivity. If your people understand the message of that book it will greatly help you implement the 22 Actions Steps found in *Making 2 + 2= 5.*

Making 2 + 2 = 5 and *Not Just for CEOs: Sure-Fire Success Secrets for the Leader in Each of Us* may be purchased from your local book supplier, or quantity purchases may be made from Irwin Professional Publishing, 1333 Burr Ridge Parkway, Burr Ridge, IL 60521. You may call Michelle Davidson at 1-800-200-2330.

When purchasing 50 or more copies, we'll supply a 14-page *Manager's Discussion Guide,* which normally sells for $2.00, to go with each book. This contains over 100 suggested questions for a manager to discuss with a front-line employee, based on the content of the book. Some examples of the 20 chapters include ways for the front-line people to streamline their jobs, learn from top performers, eliminate waste, think like an end-use customer, be a better participant in work team meetings, and prepare for their own future through further training and education.

IRWIN
Professional Publishing®

❑ Yes! Please send me *Not Just for CEOs*
   ISBN: 0-7863-0528-2 $19.95
Payment Option:

            ❑ Bill me.
            ❑ Credit card orders please call 1-800-634-3966
            ❑ Purchase Order Number _____

_____
Name   Title

_____
Organization

_____
Address   Department/Floor/Suite

_____
City/State/Zip

(_____)_____   (_____)_____   (_____)_____
Telephone   Fax   e-mail

Did you purchase this book in a bookstore? Yes_____ No_____

If yes, please indicate the store/ location. _____

What is the name and location of the bookstore where you primarily purchase professional reading materials?

_____